Patchwork of Magic
Living in a Pagan World

By Julia Day

Patchwork of Magic
Living in a Pagan World

©1995 Julia Day

ISBN 1 898307 21 0

First published Nov 1995
Reprinted May 1996

Cover design & illustration by Daryth Bastin

Published by:

Capall Bann Publishing
Freshfields
Chieveley
Berks
RG20 8TF

Tel/Fax 01635 248711

Dedication

To Jon and To Tara

and

To Grania

And to all those who have helped and to all those who
teach, both physically present and otherwise.

Acknowledgements

The many books I have read and the many ideas I have discussed. To my friends and the experiences they have shared. I just hope some of them are still talking to me!

Contents

Introduction

Why "A Patchwork Of Magic"? Because this book, like a patchwork quilt, is made up of many bits and pieces. These bits and pieces join together to make a whole, something beautiful, something that works, at least it works for me.

Perhaps I should wait to write this? Wait until I am older and wiser and until I have formed it into a coherent whole and I can sell you a package of instant wisdom and enlightenment. (!*!!!**)

What someone else writes, may hold one good idea that holds true for you, one thought that moves you onwards. Sometimes, there will be more, but just one step forward is a cause for celebration.

If I write this later, perhaps a year or two later, then I will not be writing it from here. With luck, I should have moved on a long way since then. (And I do not mean moving house!) So should you. I would be writing a different book. I hope that I am. I would not be standing in the same place or looking at the same view. My angle of vision will have changed. I might look at the same tree or stone and see it differently or see the other side. There may be something wonderful on the other side, there may be nothing, but at least I will have learnt there was nothing. A year later again and I may decide there was something after all.

What is right does not stay the same. It changes from time to time and from person to person. What is right for me now, may not be right for you.

Now, you may play with a rattle, then building bricks, then Snap, then Tarot, then visualisation then meeting minds that are not present in a physical body......

You have to decide what is right for you and know it changes.

So, there are no constants? Nothing to aim for? Perhaps you can try some of these?

Love and respect the planet on which we live.

Believe that the Divine is expressed through Nature.

Believe that divinity is expressed in both female and male forms.

Believe that the Otherworld is constantly present and intertwined with our everyday lives.

And what do you think of these?

Aim for a true expression of yourself.

Remember "And it harm none" and do your best to create what good you can. (Until someone stamps on your toe, or stabs you in the back and then also learn to defend you and yours to the best of your ability.)

Find the balance between expressing yourself and caring for others.

Increase in love and knowledge.

Move towards what seems right to you. You can do no more.

Somehow, I am not sure that that these things would react too well to being carved into stone. Not only is a stonemason unlikely to feel inspired to do it, but once something does become set in stone and has ceased to change, then it is dying.

This book is about Pagan living.

Questionnaire

It may be difficult for you to decide which branch of the magical and Pagan world suits you, or, if you attend conferences and write letters to magazines, you may not know how to describe yourself. Here is a questionnaire, which in conjunction with the descriptions later in this book, should help you with the vital task of identifying yourself and therefore, being able to display the correct badge and to know what size badge you should be wearing. As with all such things, it is important to answer the questions honestly and then to meditate upon your findings.

1. Do you prefer to drink,

      a. anything alcoholic?
      b. mead?
      c. something organic?
      d. blood?

2. Is your hair,

      a. natural in style?
      b. magenta with lime green undertones?
      c. very black, but you have to dye your eyebrows to match?
      d. you cannot really see it due to all the feathers, beads, bones, etc. in it?

3. Do you regard a goat as,

> a. something you might pass in a field on the way to some very obscure sacred site?
> b. the source of something to hang on the wall, or your staff?
> c. a fellow soul evolving alongside us?
> d. a really great prop to pose for photographs with?

4. Would you prefer to eat,

> a. something which is made to a very old and extremely complicated recipe, as long as someone else washes up?
> b. a packet of cheese sandwiches as you still have 5 miles to walk?
> c. something from Marks and Sparks, "Really dear, you can't tell the difference"?
> d. an obscure and potentially lethal sort of fungus?

5. Is your ideal form of music,

> a. drums, drums, drums, drums, drum drum drum drumdrumdumumum?
> b. whales playing pan pipes?
> c. a song your Grandmother sang, but she had forgotten half the words?
> d. the dawn chorus?

6. Would you prefer to wear,

> a. a higher vibration colour?
> b. heavy boots and lots of thick woollies?
> c. nothing?
> d. anything that will get you noticed?

7. If you believed that someone had been working magic to harm you, would you,

    a. erect a mirror to send their own harmful energies back to them?
    b. turn them into a frog?
    c. give their name and address to the "News of the Sun"?
    d. FLATTEN THEM?

8. Are your ideal working companions,

    a. the elements of Nature?
    b. yourself and one or two close friends?
    c. yourself and as many people as you can get to buy tickets?
    d. yourself and the local paper and a national paper and a foreign magazine and the B.B.C. and a helicopter.......?

9. If someone let out a series of bloodcurdling screams while you were working with them, would you,

    a. remove the point of your athame from their bottom and decide to draw the circle bigger next time?
    b. assume they had just picked up a metal incense burner with their bare hands?
    c. start thumbing through your copy of "The Exorcist"?
    d. wish they had never gone on that weekend Shaman's course?

When you have given these questions sufficient thought, you may find the following chapter which describes many different kinds of Pagan to be of help to you in discovering your true vocation (and whether I have any more idea than you about what these groups are meant to represent.)

6

Types Of Pagan

I appreciate that there are as many types of Pagan as there are Pagans, in fact, more, because people change their minds. I by no means understand all the sections and may have included some misconceptions amongst my ideas, but here are some personal observations. Apologies to all who take offence at being included. Apologies to all who take offence at being excluded.

Minimalist

They do not appear to do anything much, except go quiet for a bit. You cannot see anything going on, unless you have psychic vision of course. Afterwards, if they were successful, things seem to change.

The Traditional Witch

These can usually be recognized by the boots. They are good, thick, really serious boots that make the average fell walker look like a rank amateur. On very rare occasions, in the height of summer, traditional witches might be found wearing sandals, but then only on very short dry turf and if there are not too many other traditional witches around. (It can get very painful on the toes otherwise).

Traditional Witch

Another mark of the traditional school is the tendency to thick woollen sweaters and really heavy skirts, (in the female variety) and thick woollen socks to go with the boots. This can cause problems in the summer months, when they may be forced to remove a few layers. Occasionally robes are worn. They are generally of natural fibres, such as thick wool.....

There are occasions when no clothes may be worn, such as initiations, but traditionalists do not generally allow themselves to be photographed in such a state.

Traditional witches believe that food is important. They are almost never thin. One suspects that they will claim ANY food as traditional if they happen to have taken a fancy to it at some point. They may encourage followers, partly to pass on traditional knowledge that might otherwise be lost and which is passed down verbally from teacher to pupil over the years, but largely, to help with the washing up.

The traditional witch may well have a staff, quite possibly with a forked top. This does NOT tend to be covered in the remains of dead rabbits and chickens, though they may temporarily decorate it with flowers and seasonal vegetation. It can be used for leaning on during long conversation and also for swishing at obstructions such as nettles and brambles in a vicious manner. It, together with the boots may be used on occasions, not so much for marking out a circle, as flattening it.

They do not use scripts and so to an outsider, very little seems to happen. Sometimes the viewer is correct. Thinking up your own words and leaving empty spaces can be far more terrifying than fluffing your lines. Sometimes though the Powers take pity, or perhaps cannot stand the silence anymore and fill the gaps with inspiration.

The traditional witch generally views "And it harm none" philosophies as flimsy New Age nonsense promoted by someone who has never been in a decent magical punch up. "You leave me and mine alone or else" seems more appropriate. They are the sort of people who go into heel bars to buy a bag of hobnails, though they may not bother using a wax doll as an intermediary.

I know that the picture of a traditional witch looks rather like an amiable district nurse. All I can say is, it did not when I first drew it and I do not want to wake up to find that my (webbed) feet have been nailed to the end of the bed!

Neo Traditionalists

These are much the same as the above, except they insist upon going out in really bad weather, when the really old hands would stay at home and brew a hot toddy. Some of them also, surprisingly, react far worse than Gardnerians even to non orthodox ideas and to hints and snippets of information from other branches of the Craft.

It makes some very uneasy if someone else claims to have different traditions to them. There is a tendancy to claim that the other person is trying to impose their view of the Craft on everyone else, (even when they are not) and to retire in a huff. I therefore suspect that they feel a little insecure and need some time to settle down. A few generations should do it. The ones who are happy to admit they are new, do not tend to have the same problem.

Neo traditionalists are rather more likely to take their clothes off outdoors than the ancient traditionalists and consequently are bitten, stung and scratched more than the others which just goes to show that the Gardnerian influence creeps in everywhere.

The Hereditary Witches

For every ounce of hereditary witch, you can have several pounds of pretend ones. The pretend ones are much better at it than the real ones who do not tend to be half so impressive.

They often look very ordinary and wear ordinary clothes and have a great fund of knowledge of unwitchy things like the stars and trees and the ancient sites in their area and people seem to think they are just interested in folklore. They too have a staff, but they manage to make it look like a perfectly normal walking stick. They are not usually seen waving knives around, firstly because they have more sense, secondly because it is not necessarily traditional to use metal blades. (It depends how far back you wish to go.)

They have had "do not talk about it" drummed into the blood for so many generations that if they do mention something and ask you to keep it secret, they really mean it. Of course, some people feel that they were only being modest and so publish it anyway.

The Solitary Witch

Difficult to pin down, these may occasionally be caught in car head lights, seen climbing over a stile that leads to the middle of nowhere. They are about to embark on a fourteen mile walk to the Bouncing Laddies, a little known stone circle in the moors, normally frequented by sheep and young people doing their Duke of Edinburgh awards.

They tried joining a coven once, but were put off by some complete bunch of nutters or total time wasters. They may pronounce words oddly. This is because, although self taught by experience, they have read a few books but have no one to ask how to pronounce the words.

Hedge Witches

This group is one of those ancient phenomena that has cropped up recently. It combines several characteristics of the above groups and is based on the idea of the village wise woman. There always have been individual workers, outside of the coven system.

The book "*Hedge Witch*" by Rae Beth is important. When good, hedge witches can be extremely in-tune psychic people who are very self sufficient. When not, they may use the term to impress people, whilst covering up an appalling lack of knowledge.

The Shamans

It used to be really hard to be a shaman. You needed to talk with spirits and to have travelled in their realms, rather too closely for most peoples comfort. It is a lot easier now.....

You need a supply of various dubious substances, the most popular of which are illegal and the more experimental of which can be found growing in the countryside, some of them near birch trees, and may be procured with a certain amount of effort - if you can push all the pixies off them. These substances are consumed to bring the shamans into line with the spirit world.

Shaman

Sometimes, using this method, the shamans see the spirits of ancestors and indian guides, sometimes they see giant fluffy bunnies and sometimes something materialises like little men dressed in blue with big boots on. (The traditionalists get everywhere!)

The shaman's staff tends to be covered in feathers, beads, rabbit bones and if they are really into it a goat skull that a mate of theirs found in an antique shop in Clapham.

These people are really into dancing and drumming, I mean, really into it! Do not go near this lot with a headache unless you are prepared to dance it off, possibly the head, rather than the ache. All this drumming and dancing can be excellent for relaxing the body and reducing stress in the participants. It does not seem to do the same for the neighbours. Some folk are into chanting and singing, which can be deeply emotive and effective. It can also be absolutely appalling. Unfortunately most shamans are not shamans. I am reliably informed that real shamans work with spirits and aim to help people in the community.

There are some shamans who are actually into communing quietly with the spirits of Nature, who go out and meet real animals and are sensitive to the auras of plants, working with the Earth and the things of Earth. They do not expect a herd of buffalo to materialise in Kew Gardens and if some wild creature does show up, do not scare it half to death by beating a drum at it. They probably make far better neighbours too.

The Faery Tradition

Members of this group are characterised by the inability to spell the word "fairy".

There is a lot of personal meditation. It is about contacting the inhabitants of the otherworlds which run alongside and intermix with ours, although most people are barely aware of them, if at all.

These other inhabitants are given different names according to the point in history, the culture, or religion. They may be called, angels, spirits, guides, elves, ancestors or fairies. As with most things where there are similarities, people will strongly argue the differences.

International Conference Going Pagan

This smartly dressed set carry an attache case and their filofax and portable phone. Their clothes are the sort which never crease, even if kept almost permanently in a suitcase, (which, of course, they are.) They have black shiny shoes which look as if they should still have the price tag attached. They have a special magical aura which prevents them ever getting dirty.

Perfectly capable of organising a situation where there are hundreds of people arriving for a Pagan conference and they find the building has been double booked with the local Christian Fundamentalists, they may however panic if placed more than a couple of miles from the nearest motorway and route to an airport.

I am not familiar with these types myself, being probably considered in the straw-chewing yokel category by such sophisticates. (I still remember the look of terror in the eyes of two immaculately dressed city folk, sitting in a car, obviously lost and asking directions a whole mile from the motorway. I presume it was being so far from civilisation

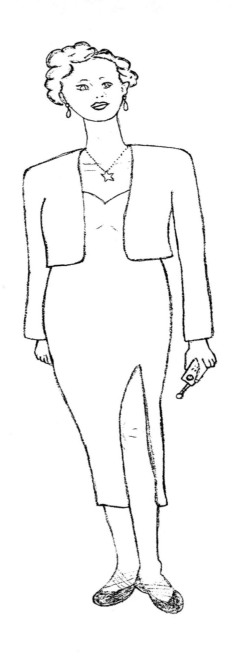

Conference Going Pagan

which scared them?) There is a small chance that I may have this group slightly confused with another city creature, the Yuppy.

Earth Mothers

This is a branch of the Craft which is pretty nearly exclusively female. If I am being politically correct, I suppose I should call them Earth Persons. It is important to be very, very large. Anyone who chooses to embark on this path, should ensure that they are <u>at least</u> thirteen stone in weight before they even start. It is possible to take special training courses which involve eating enormous amounts of cream cakes and chocolate in order to reach the necessary degree of rotundity.

Some years ago, it was necessary to wear dresses in huge floral prints which you could only get from a mail order catalogue. The advent of Eastern fashions has greatly changed this and it is now possible to float around in a voluminous cloud of tinkling cotton which can be bought in the High Street, but lacks only the guy ropes to suggest that it was otherwise destined to be a marquee.

Earth Mothers like to be surrounded by large numbers of people, preferably hungry ones. In their most natural form, this involves large numbers of other people's children, (much to the delight of exhausted parents.) Sometimes it is barely possible to tell how many children they have as the house is always full of a changing band of little ones, often accompanied by stray cats, dogs with unusual ailments that no one else wants and, if they have room, previously maltreated donkeys, rescued billy goats, etc.

It is in their nature to have an extended family who they help and care for, but problems can occur when that family turns out to be composed mostly of adults. Some are quite good at picking up lame ducks and helping them on their way. Others form a trap for themselves. They so come to rely on their role, that they start to need those "needing help" more than they are needed and so become unable to help anyone or let them go. I have known an "Earth Mother" set in motion wonderful changes in people's lives, because the person being helped, (or victim) has sorted themselves out rather than be seen to be open to such a kind (and stifling) offer.

Being an Earth Mother is something that some people grow out of. Either they no longer feel the need to be seen to mother such a huge flock as their personality no longer needs it, or they get fed up with being eaten out of house and home and decide to do some things for themselves for a change. Or they decide to go on a diet. (Of course, they may be just as kind and helpful as before, but they will no longer be the correct shape.)

There are times when a long-term Earth Mother shocks her little hatching of chicks by deciding that she has had enough of being a big soft fluffy doormat and gives the "nest" a short sharp shake, stating, "My rules from now on are...." This may greatly improve matters, but there are those who will simply move on to another ample supportive Earth Mother.

Everyone needs help at some time, but there are also times to let go on both sides.

The Northern Tradition

To some, this really just suggests the Norse Tradition, but others would class Norse, Saxon, Celtic and Pictish as Northern Tradition. The term, "Native British" is also active here.

The Norse Tradition

This is far more like the other branches of Wicca than its adherents like to admit. They have the same sort of circle, but add ice in the North. Their Gods are the Norse Gods, (e.g. Odin) who they claim are not really chauvinistic. They drink mead out of horns, which seems a plus in any religion. (Just make sure you clean them out properly after they come off the animal. Coke works well, which gives you some idea of what it does to your teeth. Don't leave it too long! Have you ever seen the experiment where they drop a real tooth into a glass of the stuff?) Norse traditionalists may have horns on their helmet and also on a very happy God of physically well endowed nature. In fact, it is a very horny religion altogether! (Historical fact, the Vikings did not normally wear horns on their helmets, possibly just on some ritual ones. I am sure many of them know that as they tend to be a well researched bunch.)

They gather their inspiration by reading Norse Sagas, runes and Hagar the Horrible cartoons. Runes have an advantage in that it is generally easier to make your own set of runes than draw your own Tarot cards. Originally a bit limited, (They all seemed to be about being hit by lightening and who would spear who to death when I tried them years ago,) they have now been updated to include spiritual development, career changes, magical healing, increase in cattle, whether you will be axed to death tomorrow, etc.

There are unfortunately some people who confuse Norse matters with Nazism, to the embarrassment and distress of others, but it is possible to find pleasanter followers too.

The Norse rites are referred to as Blots. This has nothing to do with ink, but in the past involved a great deal of being nasty to people and animals. This is frowned upon in modern circles, where tying someone to a tree, cutting them open, splaying out their ribs and removing their heart whilst they are still alive is considered rather over the top. Followers are quite into the warrior idea and so like to carry swords about in public. I am not quite sure what the women are supposed to do. I think they either wear saucepan lids on their chests or take up spinning.

Saxon

Similar to the Norse tradition, but with Saxon deities, (e.g. Woden). Plenty of mead. Some would argue that the Northern Tradition came from "Seax Wica" and owes a great deal to a book by Raymond Buckland called *"The Tree - The Complete Book Of Saxon Witchcraft"*.

Saxons do not have ice. They do not even have earth, air, fire and water around their perimeter and have a casual attitude to delineating their working area boundaries that would leave some Pagans in a cold sweat.

Celtic

Ancient British deities are honoured. There may be torc necklaces and arm rings. Some like to paint themselves blue. Lots of knotwork. Lots of mead.

It can be wonderful for artistic types and there has been a renaissance of a certain style of Celtic knotwork recently.

There are subdivisions within this group, of course! Some claim to be older, some to have got it right whilst the others are wrong and others use Irish Gaelic which means you can add lots of extra levbtters to your words or Welsh which means you can leave out the traditional vowels in your wwrdds altogedder and no one can work out how to pronounce them, even when reading silently!

There is also a great tradition of silent and meditative inner working and it is nearly impossible to avoid a crossover with the Druidic working here. (Though not all Druids are Celtic, or even Pagan.)

There is a lot of Arthurian material mixed up with some areas of the Celtic tradition. It comes in at different levels and changes emphasis according to when it is interpreted as much as to its real age. Arthur, of course, is ageless and like all good universal archetypes, keeps changing to live with the times.

Or you can simply claim to be Celtic in inspiration or by descent. This may be less fun, but you do not have to dress up in costume and can be quieter about things. I am sure it is still alright to drink mead though!

Pictish

Paint themselves VERY blue. Some nice rock carvings to copy. MORE mead I expect! There is also Pictish Heather Ale, but there is a small problem in that the recipe was lost about one thousand years ago. It suits people who like their religion to be romantic and rather Scottish. Apart from the rock carvings, there is really very little known.

Druids

Druids are different from Wiccans. I do not know how, because I have never managed to get one to make sense yet.

It takes years to become a Druid and I guess I just cannot find one who is old enough to ask. One told me that it involved him growing his hair and wearing a leather thong round his neck while another said that he had not finished the course yet.

Since I wrote that, I met a group of Druids. They were very nice people and the rite was very like a Wiccan rite, but then, since they had asked several Wiccans along as guests, that may well have been in order to make them feel at home. This was a group from the Order of Bards, Ovates and Druids.

I asked some people who have worked with Druids more and they said that Druidic energy is more gentle than Wiccan energy, may take longer to take effect and is more pervasive. They felt that Druidic working was more like Tai Chi and Wiccan energy was more like Karate!

There are many people who feel that the history of both has been extremely close and that they both contain elements of the other. There are Christian Druids and ones who's work is rather Masonic and Arthurian legend based Druids and Irish traditional ones and Fellowship of Isis Druids and hereditary ones. It would take an entire book just to examine some of them and their differences. Like many Pagan groups they are starting to hold conferences and discover that they may quite like each other, well, some of them, anyway!

'I Am a BLACK WITCH You Know' School

These wear a black polo neck or turtle neck, probably acrylic and have black hair and a goatee beard if male, gothic make up if female. They tend to be emaciated, unhealthy and display a pentagram the size of a doorknob. They may be vegetarian if the "I drink raw blood" phase failed to impress and if it helps them look more anaemic and to be a real pain to cater for. They really wish that someone would start a psychic battle with them, but most people just cannot be bothered.

Having failed to scare anything but small children and horses, they either end it all, grow out of it or turn to the press who would print the rantings of a turnip if they thought they could sell it. They make really impressive converts to fundamental Christianity as they can then get attention by claiming to know all about Satanism, but to have 'seen the light'.

The New Ager

The New Ager wears loads of crystal jewellery and displays half of the underground parts of South America in her house. She is now just starting to feel worried about the environmental damage being done with all the mining. Dress is influenced by the chakras that she is trying to excite or calm at the current moment. Prone to a form of psychedelic rainbow fatigue on occasions, she uses aromatherapy and any form of alternative healing available.

She attends courses on a huge variety of subjects and buys all the books and equipment, preferably in the most expensive form. She helps the environment by buying charity Christmas cards from people like Greenpeace.

Some of the Pagan community are now realising that we do live at the end of the 20th century and not in the Middle Ages and we may therefore be subject to the energies and new ways of expressing them at this time. It is difficult to say this too loudly however and in 1995, the term Neo-Pagan is still being used in some quarters as an insult. This will quite possibly change though. I am told that "Gardnerian" was originally used as an insult as indeed was the word "Cavalier" during the English Civil War. People have a tendency to swallow the insult and make the word into what they will, thus having the last laugh.

The New Witch

The new witch sets about the religion with a terrifying fervour. She dyes her hair purple with magenta undertones and wears matching lipstick. Both male and female forms change most of their wardrobe, building up an amazing

The New Ager

collection of tee shirts, trousers, leggings etc. all plastered with stars, signs of the zodiac, dragons etc.

The female of the species discovers ear rings the size of plates and somehow manages to wear them, whilst the male takes to winding leather thongs about various parts of his anatomy. They tend to change their name by deedpoll to something amazing and to appear in the local press quite frequently as they provide an interesting photograph of themselves doing something ritualistic with a wacking great knife.

Gardnerians and Alexandrians

I am living dangerously by grouping these two together, but it may be argued that they both came from the same source. I am not very sure about the difference, except the Alexandrians may have got a bit faster at recruiting at some point and they mix rather more High Magic, (formal stuff) into their rites. Gardnerians are named after Gerald Gardner, who came first and Alexandrians are named after Alex Saunders, though they might have been called Geraldians and Saunderians I suppose. They get very offended if you get them mixed up. There are a great many of them and this is the branch of modern Wicca best known to the press and therefore to the general public. They tend to be very brave, not just because they take off their clothes to work and include being beaten in their initiations, but they also "came out of the closet" as regards their beliefs earlier than other groups.

I asked someone (A Gardnerian.) what the differences are. It seems that one lot was founded by someone who the others think was a charlatan who said his grandmother was a witch, but that is not proved. The other group is led by

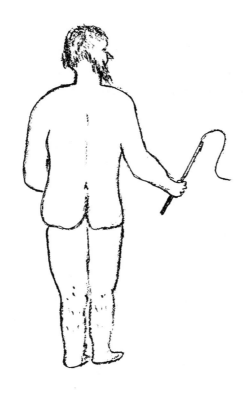

Gardnerian

someone who is also sometimes called a charlatan and who learned from an old lady, also said to be a witch and because she was alive, that proves it, except that the other chap must have had a grandmother, but that does not prove it.... I think. Basically, Gerald Gardner started it and Alex came later.

There is a tradition of initiation which records the ancestry or "pedigree" of its members. This seems strange to those groups where the last thing you would be given is a list of people's identities and to do so would be a good way to wake up in the morning sitting on a lily pad, if you were lucky. There is a coven structure which means that there should be a support structure available for training new members and it should be possible to refer to more experienced members when help is required.

They usually work indoors, which is necessitated in the UK by working in the nude or "skyclad". Far from being the mad sexual thing that the press promote, it usually has the opposite effect, humans tending to feel vulnerable rather than aroused in such circumstances. We cover ourselves so frantically most of the time, that there can indeed be a feeling of freedom with nudity. They also feel that it allows energies to radiate out from the body surface more easily, although one might be forgiven for wondering if the house walls would get in the way. This, along with bondage and flagellation during initiations is all done with the best possible taste. There are some heretical people who think that Gardner included the last two, claiming they were traditional, simply because he liked it. He did, however, bravely bring the religion into this century for many people, creating great and far reaching changes.

Like all fairly new things, it is extremely important to Gardnerians and Alexandrians that things are very old and 'right' and so they repeat things, even when they might be improved. Some of them talk about "The Book Of Shadows" as if claiming a witch "bible" and forget that there are as many of these books as there are witches. (There are possibly more witches than books as some do not have them, but you cannot be sure as some write so much.)

Despite these problems, the Craft is of course full of spiritual people who manage to express themselves and grow within it.

Rituals are scripted and performed in a theatrical manner. This makes a good show but can seem rather wasted if there are not enough of you to form an audience. The advantages of scripts are that they do not leave empty gaps when you wonder if the magic is working. The disadvantages are the same.

Farrarians

These are very similar to the above, except they are waiting for the next book.

Feminists

They believe that the world was once a wonderful rosy Heaven where women ruled. All you have to do to return to this blissful state is to ignore men whenever possible unless you are actually kneeing one in the groin. This policy has disadvantages when they decide that they want children.

Fundamentalists

These get very emotional about "The Burning Times", despite the fact that it was heretics in this country who have the real historical grudge. It is a bit like Christians having it in for lions.

Fundamentalist witches get rabidly anti Christian, which is a bit of a pity when you think that the young Jewish lad who started it all with his teaching, healing and spiritual ideas had the right idea and would have made a very good Pagan teacher if some other religious group had not got the copyright on it first. They tend to calm down once they feel more confident with themselves and their spiritual side.

Progressive Wicca (Or What Some of Us Have Been Doing All Along)

There were those who believed that you should not get stuck with a load of dogma and follow it slavishly without adding new things. They are of course, absolutely right. What they were not noticing at first is that some of us have been doing that for a long time. We have just been too polite to mention it. (P.S. I have since heard rumours that they may have worked this out for themselves after all, or alternatively, that they have helped others to recognise the point for themselves. I first wrote about this in mid 1994. I am writing this in early 1995 and it is already one of the examples of ideas in this book having to be rewritten due to people changing their thinking, which just shows how fast ideas are moving out there.)

Chaos Magic

I thought that I had covered most of the groups, until someone mentioned this. I believe it has something to do with a butterfly flapping his wings and causing a storm in a teacup. (But then I am told that is science, not magic. So that is science? What happened to the bunsen burners?)

Chaos is about primeval magic. It is also linked to turning up late to things. It is about going to talks and heckling the speaker, even if you agree with them. It is also about running out of lentil burgers at a vegan Pagan gathering and discovering that you hired two hot dog stands by mistake. Nearly all Pagan types have an affinity with this group.

I am told that really good Chaos workers are in fact extremely logical and well organized people who are capable of taking the strangest things such as Star Trek and Tolkien and turning them to magical purposes. Then of course, there are those who do not...

Chaos workers tend to develop their own systems which can seem very strange indeed. Some are Shamanic, others love ritual more. Some are not even Pagan I believe, but since I have spent some time trying to find out what exactly they do and even, (shock, horror) read a book about it, I am not going to leave them out because of that!

Ecological Pagans

Difficult to classify, this group do not tend to have a great deal of time for rituals, though they may well stop to talk to a tree now and then. Some can be found up to their knees in mud, helping to unblock canals and shifting rubbish from natural areas or helping children to appreciate the wonders of the world. If they raise the Earth's energies and ask for spiritual help, it is because they have a need. They do not raise power just to impress. They do it to help themselves or others and do not waste energy, feeding any excess back to the planet and believing in giving and exchanging rather than taking all the time. They may become physically involved in attempts to save parts of the countryside, ancient sites and woodland. Often vegetarian, they tend to recycle anything possible.

Being quietly spiritual, they believe in rolling their sleeves up and doing what they can to improve at least a tiny part of the world. They do their best at "and it harm none" until they find that people trample all over them and then discover that you have to stand up for yourself in a world which allows evil to manifest, so they just do their best whilst learning to defend themselves when necessary. Unbelievably, despite the almost childish simplicity of this philosophy, many succeed in their aims.

Conclusion

The author would like to suggest that she has now left the country and is living under an assumed name and has several friends who are good at turning people into frogs and once knew someone with an Italian surname who's dad might have been on good terms with the mafia.

Well, seriously folks, now which section do you fit in? Quite possibly more than one and they may change as your beliefs alter and develop and of course you may have an affinity with one of the groups that I have failed to mention. (It is pretty dangerous to offend everyone, after all!)

There are, or should be, as many groups as there are Pagans. Each of you should be following your own path and your own ideas. Yes, I know I have poked fun at several groups of people, but it was not their spiritual beliefs that I wished to make fun of. I just wanted to point out that in searching for something, we fall into patterns of behaviour, clothing, beliefs etc. which may for a time help us on our way. They can also, however, become a trap. It is possible to get all the clothes and get all the fancy gadgets and not even have begun to discover what you are really seeking. The door to this, of course, is inside yourself.

It is sad to watch a person copy a way of dressing, or even a personal mannerism, hoping that somehow it will help them on their way, especially when the one they are copying is, in reality, as lost as they are.

I am not saying that it is wrong to enjoy dressing up a bit. Certainly not! There should be more fancy dress parties in life! It can be a great release to break the dress patterns demanded by your family, your occupation, your friends, but do not become trapped in yet another rut. Of course, if you change too often though, you are liable to become very broke, very confused or a very messy dresser! After a while, the changes may have to go on inside. But then, as things do start to happen, you should eventually get to the stage where you do not need to wave the flags any more. You will also not need to attach labels to yourself as you will have more confidence in what you are doing and having jumped in the water a few times, you discover that the labels tend to come off in the wash anyway.

Ritual According To Pagan Types

Now each group would tend to approach the same problem in many different ways, so I intend to attempt to give some examples of different approaches to the same challenge.

This also gives me the opportunity to lose a few more friends and ensure that any Pagan gatherings I attend will have to be in disguise. (I know! I will go as a police helicopter!)

Seriously though, I really do believe that our police force is going Pagan. Do you know, I was at Avebury this Summer Solstice Eve and this friendly helicopter kept circling the pub where a small group of people were quietly eating, drinking, talking, singing etc. and then 4 BUS LOADS of police turned up, which just shows they hate to miss a good Pagan party!

So, if you really want to get into all those Pagan sites at the major festivals, JOIN THE POLICE FORCE!

The example I will give is a healing rite.

Minimalist

It means that you leave out as much clutter as possible and leap straight into action. Sitting, lying or standing, think of a circle around yourself. You may wish to envisage the elements. Think of the person you wish to help, think of the energy rising within you and/or entering you, send the energy, thinking of the person becoming well, close off the contact between the two of you, settle your own energies, thank the elements and say goodbye if you called them and come out of it. Dissolve the circle. Have something to eat and drink, bringing yourself back to Earth.

It tends to work, but it is very boring to watch.

Traditional Approach

First, oil your boots. Second, air the moth ball smell out of your clothes. Choose a site, (one that is difficult to reach is best) and then head for it getting someone else to carry the hamper. Comment on all the elementals etc. charging around.

Set up a simple circle, preferably waving your hands around in various odd patterns. Mutter a few words, get to the food and drink bit, throw most of it on the ground as a libation, get someone else to clear up and go back.

Objects such as a forked staff (stang) and sickles may be used, but I am not going into all that here.

Neo Traditionalists

Much the same, but go out in worse weather and sometimes undress. They frequently work alone and cannot claim to be so ancient, so have to carry their own picnic.

Hereditary Approach

This lot will do what they choose to do unless they are doing what their Grandmother told them to do. They will probably do it alone and quietly and with something very simple and inexpensive, if they need anything at all. A little later, they might ask if the person is feeling better.

Alternatively, if they make a CLAIM of being hereditary, it will all be more public and impressive. It may even work.

Solitaries

They will work very quietly, alone and in a way that they have found works for them.

Hedge Witch

Similar to the above and the meditation on healing may be fairly easy to arrange, but if she takes the hedgerow idea seriously she may be hampered in certain rural areas by the tendency to reduce huge tracts of the landscape into featureless chemical deserts.

Useful things like comfrey may well have to be grown in the garden, because, not only is one unable to find a hedgerow, let alone useful plants in it in some areas, but it does not bear thinking about what has been sprayed on the few herbs you can discover.

Shamanic Approach

This is much more fun! Get lots of animal skulls and put them on your stick and round your neck and on your belt and anywhere else they will fit. Take some natural substances, such as mushrooms of the sort that do not come from greengrocers and probably something that those Pagan police would love to know about and start hitting those drums! And drum! And drum! etc. You can let out odd yodelling sounds, which are supposed to sound Red Indian, or like a drunk on the London Underground. Start trying to count the six foot high fluffy white bunny rabbits which are revolving around your head. Just before you go off to be 'orribly sick, wonder if you have forgotten something.

Faery Tradition

This could involve quiet, personal meditation and making contact with a non physical helper. It can involve the belief that someone will be listening, even if you are failing to see or hear them. This can be extremely effective, depending on two things. You have to ask something reasonable and they must feel that it is right for them to help you achieve it. You also have to accept the other side's timescale, which can seem very drawn out sometimes. (It can also be alarmingly fast.)

International Conference Going Pagan

They may organise a seventy person rite at a major international gathering in another country, but it will not take place for another three months. Or, they would love to fit you in but sadly they are just about to fly to South America to visit a little known spiritual community who are holding a gathering so cannot do it. Or, they could just squeeze you in for a working breakfast appointment sometime next week, but could you please phone them on the mobile when you have covered the first hundred miles of your journey, to check that they are still in the country?

Earth Mother

Food is probably the answer to the problem. Plenty of it! Also, the good ones can be marvellous if you want to leave the children with someone for a month or so because you are feeling a bit under the weather. They may also be very good at things which need a sympathetic listening ear. The person being helped must work out for themselves though, when to make their escape, unless they choose to risk their adult independence disappearing totally.

Northern Tradition

Norse

Much the same as the others, but get in plenty of mead and remember to add ice. (You can wear horns too, I think.)

Saxon

Like the above, but Saxon and without ice. Extremely simple boundaries.

Celtic

Plenty of mead and possibly knotwork, but without the ice. Psychic ability may be expected to be "in the blood". A lot may happen with little physical activity to demonstrate it. If it works, things change. Energies change too.

Pictish

Unable to start the rite, because they are still covering themselves in intricate designs in blue eye liner. Alternatively, they started early and have managed to get themselves covered in minute spirals, or have speeded things up by using a stencil and a spray can. Unfortunately, one of them is experimenting with a "Heather Ale" recipe that suggests it originally contained shamanic, narcotic mushrooms, so no sense out of them for the rest of the night!

Druids

You can either wander about wearing a bedsheet and making very long speeches in Welsh, or you can do something very similar to the others, but hope no one notices the similarities. It was once possible to wander around in the middle of Stonehenge and sometimes appear on television for a "fifteen second look at the loony, we have run out of serious news" bit, but now it is very difficult to seem dignified when involved in a rugby scrum with the police. (Especially the officers they bus in from outside who seem to enjoy a little Pagan bashing as an alternative to patrolling streets in armoured vehicles, or whatever else they use in cities nowadays. You have to remember that some of the local P.C.s maybe wandered down there to watch the sun rise themselves once. This can be difficult to visualise if someone is standing on your head whilst wearing size 15 boots at the time.)

Some Druids have very nice ceremonies, which are very loving and spiritual and very Wiccan. (But some get upset if you mention it.) Whether Druids came from Wicca or Wicca came from the Druidic ways (or whether it hatched out of an egg or appeared as a fully fledged chicken) does not seem to matter when people get on with something that works. (Other Druids, believe it or not, are Christian, some will work with Arthurian characters and the list continues in its variety. I guess it is fair to say it varies from great shows of complicated ritual to inner workings.)

Black Witch

Healing? HEALING!!??

New Age

A wonderful chance to buy even MORE crystals! You can then charge them up with healing energy and pop them off in the post. Simple! (It may be an idea to start bulk buying the crystals though.) You can wear certain colours and think complementary healing colours too, though it is a real bother if pink does not suit you and can be annoying if people keep asking you to sign Barbara Cartland novels all the time.

The New Recruit

Here is a wonderful chance to tell all your friends and buy something new for your wardrobe! Perhaps you could get the local press to come and I am sure the police have a spare helicopter or two! Make sure you take some really good props. If you are using a real billy goat, pack plenty of air freshener and that aftershave which has been sitting in the bathroom for all those years.

Gardnerians and Alexandrians

There may be a long lead up time as someone has to write the script. If one of the members has recently felt inventive regarding rituals, there may be a quite involved play about some Greek deity or Egyptian or Abyssinian or some lesser known South American Fruit Bat Deity and it will need enough people to play all the parts and leave some to watch. The dressing up box will contain all sorts of interesting things, all designed to leave uncovered the bits that most people normally try to keep hidden. The Alexandrian one will contain more High Magic, which means it has more complicated bits. I expect the two groups could easily recognise the difference between the two sorts of rites. I am not sure that I could.

There is just as much of a chance of healing being successful as with any other system which happens to be fortunate enough to be being worked by the right people.

Farrarian

Read the books.

Feminist

All female cast, with lots of soul searching. Women were always best at healing and the problem was probably caused by a man anyway.

Fundamentalist

Too busy writing a book about Christian oppression.

Progressive

Like the rest, but with some bits added and some bits changed.

Chaos

"I thought YOU were bringing the candles?"

"What do you mean, it was last night?"

"Oh, you meant THAT sacred site?"

"I thought North was that way?"

"My clock started running backwards."

"You could go and ask the pub to give us some salt." (They did too, those lovely people. Then someone forgot to take the bowl away afterwards. The next morning, there were a lot of happy cows and a very well licked bowl.)

"Sorry, we didn't bring the wine....we bought some toilet rolls instead." (This was, to be honest, for a meal rather than a rite, but it gives the general idea. It also leaves me wondering if they were a little worried about the quality of the food!)

The majority of the above quotes are based upon things that people have really said, (probably hundreds of times.)

"Did you see Star Trek last night?"

"Waiter, there is a butterfly in my teacup."

Ecological Pagans

If you are unlucky, they will just have read a book on herbalism and will give you a pretty bottle containing a mixture of lemon balm, hemlock and deadly nightshade. Experienced ones will do whatever they think will help the person get better, including sending flowers and a get well card!

Well, I think I have insulted most groups fairly now, though in line with human nature, most of us may feel that the criticism is justified, except when it comes to our own group and then of course, it is complete nonsense!

There are many different paths to the same desired end. It does not matter which label people allow themselves to be identified with (and some refuse to be labelled) the fact is that many of them will indeed try to help, using many different methods and with varying degrees of success. A highly ritualised approach will reap great benefits for one group, whilst another individual may help the healing process with a few twigs or a moment's concentration.

There are of course, those who help by using a wide variety of approaches. The result is not always success, not necessarily because we used the wrong method, or did not try hard enough, but because we are trying to heal the wrong thing. Perhaps the illness is just the symptom of something deeper? Sometimes, sadly, people are not meant to get well. Either, they have a lesson to learn from their condition in this life, or their allotted time span is up. They may even give to others, by their example of dealing with difficulties and their own death. There are people who have found themselves deeply touched by another person's bravery, strength and even humour when facing long illness and death.

Some work to gain too. I do not just mean the "Brownie Points" or good karma that many feel is gained by good works, but they gain an understanding of magical working and of what can and cannot be done.

Sacred Space

Most books contain a section on drawing or visualising your magic circle. The description varies from taking up great sections of the book, to just a paragraph. Of course, the fact is, you can make the process as complicated as you like. If you enjoy drama and paraphernalia, then go for it! If you need to repeat a set of actions to convince yourself that it is there, then do it. You may find a series of repeated actions helps you to calm down into a working state of being. It can be a great calmer of the mind, like a Buddhist raking gravel and like the mind going to a wedding, we enjoy a little special occasion!

There are times though, when the time, materials and effort needed to set up, can actually exhaust you, to the point of not being able to perform the work. Is it a special occasion, or does something just need doing, or someone need helping, now?

When you create a circle, you are making a space in the non physical world. You simply have to believe, know or feel that it is there. This may be done by visualising, or by simply thinking to yourself, that it is there. You may also choose to draw it physically in the dust if you are outside or to mime drawing it inside.

Also, do remember that it is a sphere. I know that this is said many times, but I have met many people who have read all sorts of things and been on courses with famous people and they still do not know this, or forget it! You are surrounded, not just by the compass points around you, but also by above and below, in traditional terms, "Sky above and Earth below."

It can be great fun learning to visualise spheres. The mind plays tricks and tries to make sense of it all using its everyday experience. You might find yourself going round in a goldfish bowl for instance. Others can only visualise a sphere by constructing it a bit at a time, by the time the last part is created, the first part has dissolved! There are also those who forget the top or the bottom (or both) and those who suffer from claustrophobia! Whilst thinking about the sphere passing through the earth beneath your feet, you may become aware of the Earth and even feel that you are dropping down and moving through it. Disconcerting though this can be at first, it can be a valid experience in itself.

This then is the basic working area. Different religious beliefs and magical systems then add to the sphere. Guardians are called to protect the circle. These vary. In High Magic, people may call, indeed, order and command angels, demons etc. Now, it seems to me, that the majority of these beings are a great deal more knowledgeable and powerful than me and if me, then others too, else why do we need their help? The idea of trying to make demands on them makes me feel distinctly uncomfortable.

In the pantheistic and Pagan beliefs, representatives of the physical elements of fire, water, earth and air are invited or requested to attend and help. Note, *requested*. The aim is to work with the natural forces, not club them over the head, drag them home and then expect them to be friends with you. Also, always remember to say goodbye to each element at the end of the rite and to THANK them. It is amazing what people can receive from the psychic and spiritual realms and forget to say thank you. We forget so often in ordinary life, indeed, sometimes we are quite unaware of the help. Let us remember it here.

Also, having a bad tempered elemental around is no joke. If an elemental has been trapped, it usually has only one way of letting you know. When all your electrical goods fail and the fire will not light properly, or the washing machine, the radiators and the roof all start leaking, perhaps you have an unwelcome guest. An apology, if deserved and a polite invitation to leave, may be on the cards! You can help this by providing a little help, related to the element involved. Burn a candle, light incense, pour water, bring in a bowl of earth. Then invite the elemental to enter its own element. Just let your childish imagination work, it will know what to do.

Due to someone else's less than wonderful behaviour, we once had elementals trapped in our house. The vacuum was trying to catch fire. I took it over to the fire place, lit some paper in the grate and said, "There you are little elemental, off you go!" It was childish I know, but on that occasion it worked. On others, sadly, the machine has had to go off and be mended!

The elements are physically there already, what we are doing is calling up our psychic awareness of their presence and asking them to stay with us for a time. Sometimes someone may force an elemental's attendance, rather than invite them. How would you feel? We must always leave them free to go their own ways afterwards.

Another important reason for taking down a circle at the end of working, in addition to freeing elementals and not being a psychic litter lout, is that the personal energies, which have been given to set up the circle, should be returned to the individuals involved. Anyone responsible for setting up a circle, must also be responsible for taking it down. The lessons attached to not doing so oneself can be longwinded and uncomfortable.

The traditional positions for the elements in modern Wicca are as follows, Earth in the North, Air in the East, Fire in the South and Water in the West. The Northern tradition includes ice. Older British traditions vary and may call on four winds rather than four elements or four trees which then represent the four elements. Some North American traditions use different compass positions and they can vary around the world. If you have a great lake or the sea to one side of you, it would be crazy to insist on fire being there and try to invoke water elsewhere!

It can be pleasing to place physical representations of the four elements at the four quarters of the circle. If you are working outside, however, you have the elements already there. You do not need a bowl of water if you are by a stream and an oak tree may stand sentinel over the North.

You may wish to bring something to represent fire. It is not good manners to burn great holes in the ground and leave them littered with rubbish and half burnt logs. Some sacred sites, such as the Rollright Stones, have notices asking you not to, though there was still a great burnt area there when I visited it. At most a discrete scorched patch is permissible. This will allow other Pagans to give sidelong glances to each other and to nod knowingly and recognise that others have been there. I do hope that it is not giving away too many secrets to say that I know of one traditional group who use a metal dustbin lid. (If I wake up with webbed feet and a liking for lily pads one morning, I shall know that I offended

somebody.) A portable barbecue could function as camouflage too! A candle or oil lamp will do. The trouble is, that fire can be so exciting!

We felt that we had to have a fireplace in our home, so we had a fireplace and chimney added to our house: the original ones had been removed. It seemed vital to us and friends love it too. The firemen were quite good too, when the chimney caught fire, with flames shooting out of the chimney like a great firework and only dying down just before they arrived so that they could not find the house. They took their boots off, left it cleaner than they found it and even refrained from axing the front door down! They said that throwing water on the fire had helped as it sent steam up the chimney. The salt, they said, had done nothing. Personally, I think that the old advice of throwing salt on the fire is probably the last folk memory of exorcising a fire elemental.

We are starved, most of us, of living wood fires and so they hold quite a fascination. People find themselves building something big enough to roast several of their predecessors on. Edward Woodward and "The Wicker Man" have got a lot to answer for. Also, so many people just do not know about building fires when they have a site that allows it. One group I was with were instructed to use only dead wood. One started hacking at the nearest living tree like a mad thing and a girl picked a little bunch of ever so pretty pussy willow blossoms to add to the fuel pile! The Scouts and Girl Guides may not have been intended to train Pagans, but they have their uses. The next morning, there was so much unused wood, that it had to be cleared with a van.

But, I digress. How big should a circle be? There are all sorts of rules according to what you read or who talks to you. (It is much more impressive to have verbal lessons from someone, even if they are just one chapter ahead and have to keep diving into the bathroom to check the next bit in the book.) You can measure it in feet or even megalithic yards, or paces. You can use pieces of cord to measure it out. You can base its size upon the diameter of your cauldron. It just does not sound right in metres though!

In fact, the great secret, I think, is that you make it as big as you need. (Or as big as your lounge, or as large as the patch between the nettles, the ditch with an iron bedstead in it, the oak tree and the brambles.) There is no point making it huge. It takes more out of you to maintain and becomes "thinner" eventually. Anyone who has read a book saying "9 feet across" and tried to fit a baker's dozen into that and dance without kicking the candles over will know what I mean. I think that 9 feet was originally enough for one organized magician, not a dozen shambling or gambolling maniacs with an altar and a cassette player loaded with North American stomping songs. You will not get your wing feathers round much of the universe in that little space!

Within that sacred space, you are literally in another world and it is a marvel to so many people as they step into it for the first time and feel the difference. It is hard for many to say goodbye and thank you and dissolve it when the time comes.

A protective sphere has similarities. People who travel along psychic paths must expect that at some time they will need to protect themselves. A sphere is envisaged about oneself, strengthening one's natural protection. It moves about with you. You can do the same with a vehicle, though it can be tricky to envisage at first. It can also be seen about your home and garden and even place of work. You can put it round others that you love too. However, you must remember that you will stretch your ability thinner and thinner and can start to become very tired. Trying to protect someone who rejects your help, or is in some way draining energy, will exhaust you very quickly and you will have to break that link. It can be a hard lesson to learn about your own limitations.

People give different instructions for seeing these spheres, suggesting white, violet or pale blue colours. Choose what seems right to you. You can add crystals or imaginary mirrors to it if you wish. It is your imagination! I even mounted a lazer gun on a boundary protection once, when I was really being pushed! It's disc gathered anything bad coming in and then fired it back!

Hopefully, your sacred space will be used for much calmer and happier things. Perhaps its special feeling will help you to meditate or to use some form of divination or to gain inspiration. It is an area within which you can build up power to help with healing or consolidate your own energies in a demanding world. It is within your sacred space, too, that you will wish to meet the Powers, the energies of Earth and the Spiritual energies. You may meet these outside of a circle too.

After a time, you find that sacred space starts to be all over the place! Sacred space stops being a physical spot and becomes a state of mind. Someone travelling astrally can take the protection with them. In the same way, the sacred space is something which becomes part of you and part of everyday living. You still have to remember not to step out in front of buses though! I am not certain what shape a psychic sphere becomes when underneath a bus, but I think it would be accompanied by an unhealthy amount of red.

Initiation

What is initiation? It is, "to begin", to "set on foot" and to "instruct in the ways of" according to my "*Oxford School Dictionary*", that well known tome of occult meanings.

The last meaning would certainly suggest the helping hand of a teacher or guide and it is easier to have one which is physically present. But, of the first and second meanings, "to begin" and "set on foot", surely, it is possible to start a journey alone? For many things which are of worth and involve advancement along psychic and spiritual lines, being self sufficient to a greater degree is what much of it is about.

There are strong arguments flying around at the moment about people being initiated by others as opposed to those who "self initiate". Some feel that there is no such thing as self initiation and everyone needs to work with and learn from another person, only being accepted into the Craft by another already in it.

What I generally mean by initiation, is some form of welcoming rite to a new member of the Craft. It is a form of rebirth. There is an oath of commitment and of responsibility. Some of the traditional paths may involve several initiations, which change as the initiate ages. Some of the older paths involve sexual induction.

What I will discuss here, relates mostly to modern Wicca and older versions of the Craft, where there is a belief in something being passed on. Other Pagan groups, Shamanic workers for instance, may consider initiation to be a completely different process which need not involve other people being physically present.

Initiation varies so much from group to group that I do think it a good idea to ask beforehand what initiation involves! There will always be certain elements of surprise, but someone should be able to give you a rough idea at least, even if it is just to say "No" to a series of questions. You should be able to ask, "Who will be there?" "Where will it be?" "What should I wear?". With initiations carried on everywhere from living rooms to Neolithic Sites and with some involving ritual flagellation whilst other groups would collapse in side-splitting hysterical laughter at the idea, there is quite a range! You should always feel comfortable and that you trust the people, otherwise, walk away.

There should always be a good period of time between meeting people and considering whether you might wish to be initiated by them. Traditionally, you should know each other and, in some traditions, been learning about the Craft for a year and a day, (Samhain, the old "day between the years" was the reason for so many fairy tales being based on "a year and a day"). Some believe that you should wait that long after having asked, which can seem a long time if you took your time deciding in the first place!

Some paths, including Gardnerian and Alexandrian, involve three initiations. The first, represents entry to the Craft, the second, the ability to work for oneself and the third seems to vary, though some associate it with the ability to form and run a coven independently. The third is often taken by people when they themselves feel ready and therefore in some circles, where a sense of being important has taken hold, there can be quite a sense of taking Brownie badges sometimes, as people pop up to third degree overnight like mushrooms! Such people forget though that responsibilities are accepted with initiations and they may find that they have taken on more than they bargained for.

I feel that initiation involving other experienced people is a good thing. To have kind, wise people to help you, to have the friendship and support of others with similar views, these are excellent things to have. I find myself so annoyed with the almost elitist attitudes that some people are advocating at the moment though, that I find it hard to remember these things!

What about all the people who cannot find someone to initiate them? I know, the "teacher will come along when the time is right." Try telling that to someone who has waited twenty years. They may feel like thumping you!

To have someone who can pass on both knowledge and experience is wonderful. (Assuming of course, that you have a wonderful person helping you. Sadly, not always the case.) It seems also, that the belief in Apostolic succession is not just confined to some sections of the Christian Church. The trouble is, it was used there to keep political, rather than spiritual power in check. That side of things has to be watched. Ego will out sometimes! Initiation is not an excuse to play power games, well, not the power of ego, anyway.

Passing the power on is a gift of giving. Some groups believe that at a later initiation, which takes place after the first introductory initiation, access is given to the entire history of power and knowledge within the group by such an act. That is not given lightly.

The sad fact is that there are also a very large number of people out there who are only too ready to play the role of the great white chief to as many as they can get to "follow" them. There are also those who usurp and steal the power of individuals that they get into their grasp.

There are those who refuse to give out any information until someone is finally initiated, at which point, they find that they have given their oath to goodness knows what. Some dribble out their meagre amounts of wisdom over as many years as they can, holding back the students who would have shot past them like a sky rocket, had they not placed their trust in the wrong person and been honourable enough to stay faithful to their oath to an unworthy individual.

I even have a friend who turned up to her first group with a friend who had asked her along for moral support, to find the press there and realised to her disbelief, that she was being "initiated" by a person she had never met before. Her photo was taken and unknown to her, her address was given to a newspaper reporter, who turned up at her house. Without her permission, in fact, despite attempts to stop it, her photo is held on file as that of a witch and regularly appears in media publications, even years later.

Good job she got properly initiated, wasn't it? I am delighted to say she went on to meet far more pleasant people after that.

I will say again, the help and support of good teachers is invaluable, but ego and personality have a lot to answer for. Some people have paid a very heavy price for their initiation. If you seek initiation, be very careful who you trust. It is better to wait than spend years sorting out a mess.

All this it seems, is prefered by some to not having the initiation.

Many, of course, turn their back on all Pagan matters following such experiences. Others avoid the problems by daring to self initiate.

As an alternative, it is possible to hold a very deep, meaningful ceremony of self dedication, or an affirmation. In this, a person gives a personal vow which is between themselves and their view of deity or may be witnessed by their partner or friends if they have already come together in their beliefs. Then, if there is a wish to be initiated by another person one day, there need not be any feeling of rushing. There is plenty of time to find the right person. Your psychic and Pagan life does not grind to a complete halt just because you are not initiated.

The things which are of value, are the things that are going on in your heart and the changes that are taking place on all levels because of your decision. You can state those things which you wish to be and to learn and do and they all have real importance, even without a crowd of others and without dramatic ceremony.

Here is another great truth, which like most of them, comes over as something very simple and is therefore easily ignored and forgotten.

Initiation is not just something which takes place on the physical level.

There are people who would not get the message if a kipper swam past them at the bus stop or a flock of albino ostriches landed on their heads. If however, someone, preferably with a good lineage, like being descended from Rasputin's Aunty and some famous author's hamster, conducted a rite in fantastic robes with as many complicated permutations of candle colour as possible without actually melting the carpet, they would be impressed. They would feel properly "done". (And some of them are, too.)

Initiation involves changes on the inner level.

There are those who say that they have been initiated, but not by any physically alive person. They are normally disbelieved of course. It is not simple to check. Genuine initiations of this kind involve inner changes to the person involved. They are displayed though in what that person is and does, for sensitive people to see. There of course, we have it. Some people, who consider themselves very important, are unable to see it and that unsettles them.

Real initiations take place on and are part of the other levels of existence. For a physical ceremony to have meaning, it must also be registering change, or at least the start of change, upon all levels of the individual's existence.

There are initiations on the astral and sub astral planes. There are initiations of the spirit. They take place all the time. Here is the bit that will really annoy a lot of people. They do not just take place with those initiated into the Craft, or indeed, with those who consider themselves to be on an occult path. They happen throughout life to everyone. It is just that most people do not recognise them.

Unlike many of the other initiations, they are not timetabled by people either. They happen in life, frequently as part of everyday life and it is only afterwards that someone realises what has happened.

Often, there have been very troubled times, which may or may not involve psychic or spiritual awareness and as a result, the individual has grown and become stronger.

How can someone know that such an initiation has taken place? Besides having overcome a major challenge, there are often signs. These may be something which might seem quite ordinary, perhaps an encounter with an animal, but then, something happens which takes it out of the everyday routine. If the message still has not dropped into the initiate's mind, someone may explain it. Even a complete stranger may hold a message for someone. Once you start to interact with the other planes as part of your ordinary life, the oddest "coincidences" and "synchronicity" will become part of normal living.

This is the part where one might expect a list of signs and what they mean. "If you dream you hear the cuckoo your sweetheart will prove a coquette" says "The Victorian Book Of Dreams." "A mole on the nose, shows that the person will have good success in the most of his or her undertakings." I suppose that a wart on the nose will denote that the person is a witch, a reincarnation of Oliver Cromwell or has a problem with personal hygiene.

I am not going to give you a list of signs. There are some which seem to be recognised as common symbols and if they help you, you will find them in other books. Others though are very personal. Signs which have meant things to me are just that, personal and private.

I will give you an example though. A bird entering and flying round the house is feared by many people. Some say it is a sign of death. I have found it to be a time of change, although often involving difficulties, ultimately, for the better. The "Death" card in Tarot represents change, for whenever something new happens, something old has to die and be replaced. The entry of a wild bird also often happens when there has been a major change to the house, perhaps an extension and then it seems like a kind of blessing.

If there are certain events that crop up in your life and seem to have more than usual significance, then it is worth keeping a record of them. This includes unusual dreams. Some people record all their dreams. It depends how much time you have and how interesting they are, I guess! If you start to learn to decode them though, you have an invaluable resource to help you on your path. (And I do not just mean trying to get the next Derby winner!)

If you cannot understand something alone, then just ask for help. (That unfashionable word, "pray" surfacing here.) It is funny how someone will suddenly find themselves telling you a story which gives you exactly the clue you needed, or a book that you are browsing through in a shop will fall open at just the right page. Or, as has just happened now, a friend phones up with some interesting information which adds to a point I was thinking about.

If you are lucky enough to meet the right person, who you can trust to carry out your initiation, then you are a most fortunate person. It is and should be, a wonderful gift. There are initiations though, which do not involve other people which are nevertheless very real. You can consider yourself fortunate if you experience these too. Just be honest about what you have experienced, but know when to keep quiet. Some people are not worthy of your honesty.

There have always been those who have learnt from one person and worked mostly alone, or who have learned from several sources, or even have taught themselves from direct contact with Nature and their own inner guidance and guides. Someone who sees initiation simply as a set of rites with the correct person officiating in a set structure, has a lot to learn. You are better learning alone for a while, rather than tying yourself to the wrong person. Remember too, some of these arguments come down to nothing more than a problem with words. What one person means by "initiation" may simply differ from your interpretation.

The Coven Leader

So you want to make it big in Wicca? Well, forget all about this self development nonsense and become a coven leader. If you can get several covens to hive off, then you have really made it! If you are a Gardnerian High Priestess,(or is that Farrarian?) you can wear these cute little garters with horseshoe buckles on too! It is easy to find a supply of these, just use wedding cake decorations!

Get a soap box! Get a pedestal! Get a grandmother who was in the Craft, or failing that, an elderly aunt who did not go to church too often. Make sure that you DO NOT tell anything of worth to anyone and make them promise not to tell what little they do glean to anyone else, (as you are already writing a book on the subject).

Get people to take very complicated oaths that do not quite fit in with commonsense and then get really miffed when they come to you a while later and say it is not what they were hoping for.

You need an impressive personality and an ego the size of a battleship. You need to stop learning and repeat things that you never understood in the first place. Follow them, year after year, including the spelling mistakes, the ketchup stains and the bit where Michael dropped the burning hot wax on his......

"Stop! Stop! Stop! Hold on a minute! This is not what it is about!"

"Well, I am sorry, but for a lot of people, it is!"

I knew two young people, one of whom was initiated and then abandoned by circumstance and by someone who thought very little beyond himself. So they set to and did their best to learn and good luck to them. But then they felt that they had to form a coven. So they became a High Priest and High Priestess and they initiated a friend. Next thing I hear is the exhausted would-be High Priestess saying, "I initiated her, but now she won't do anything I tell her!" I hope I am forgiven for mentioning it.

The trouble is that the idea of personal power can be a great draw to the ego. People begin to live a role and where others try to live that role, a caricature appears and more people start to follow the caricature. They start to think that if they behave in that way, they must be getting it right, they must be succeeding.

I have seen a young person, new to Paganism, desperate to learn, copy the personal mannerisms of another following an attempted working. What was so sad, was that the working had been going very wrong. The impressive movements of one were quite unrelated to the psychic impressions, hard work and distress being experienced by others in the group. It is the actor who will impress the new and the young.

More than once, I have seen gestures and heard descriptions and flourishes carried out by a performer, whilst others quietly visualised and created what was needed.

Then there is the question of 'letting go'. How can someone let go of a member of their coven if that member does not feel right or feels ready to spread their own wings, if the leader does not have the numbers to keep up their group? For they become trapped in their own stereotype. What are they without it? If they are lucky and realise what has happened, then they may find themselves standing at the bottom of a long staircase, but this time with the chance of the vision to start moving up.

This does not mean that all people should work alone, or that people should not teach, just do not get caught up in the false structures, the over-cosy "I have arrived safely" feeling. It is not about arriving, it is about travelling.

There is the feeling of coming home, felt for many at initiation, or their first time in a circle. There is that feeling often when someone finds out about Wicca or Paganism or any other religious path which has something to teach them. That is not a point of stopping though, it is a time of beginning, of placing the feet on a path, of taking that first step that will cover a thousand miles and keep going.

Another great rule is:

DO NOT STOP!

Sometimes, you need a rest, sometimes you go too fast. Your job and your loved ones have needs and your body must be able to keep up. You do need to rest and on occasions, a place may seem nice for quite a long time, but the idea is to travel forward.

You waited a long time for your physical incarnation. You worked hard for it You went through birth and nappies and not being allowed to eat all the crisps in the house and cross country running and pimples and buying a house and wrinkles and.....just to be here again, so that you could go on learning in your physical form.

So make the most of it. Just be ready to notice some of those little side tracks which can slow you down. The ego can do a lot. It is there to help you maintain your idea of self, but it also causes problems. Even when you might be quite advanced, it is there, riding a bicycle with no hands, balancing on one foot on top of a wall, saying, "Look at me! Aren't I spiritually advanced! Wheee!"

We need to work with others and learn from them and as time goes on, we will all hopefully add something to other people's understanding and lives, but watch out for that old power game, both as a would-be pupils, who find themselves learning little except a lesson about egos, or as a teacher.

I hate to admit it, but I have felt it, that feeling of power before a group of people who mostly do not know what you are really capable of. The urge to pose. I was rescued from that, even though I did not know that there were those there with real psychic ability. I forgot the one short line I had to say, (I hoped they thought it a dramatic pause, but Jon knew I was desperately trying to remember,"Hail and Welcome!"). I also felt the terrific exhaustion of a group that had set themselves too hard a task, due to my own inexperience and had to fight to pull us through. I learnt a lot. I decided to keep my hands on the handlebars of the bicycle.

Festivals

The majority of people thinking about the festivals will think of the modern regular eight festival wheel of the year. This consists of Beltaine, Lughnassadh, Samhain and Imbolc with the second cycle of Midsummer, Midwinter (Yule) and the Spring and Autumn equinoxes. Not all of these festivals will have the same strengths of meaning for individuals. The four strongest are usually felt to be Beltaine and Samhain and Midsummer and Midwinter.

Many people now think that the only system is one which has eight festivals which neatly divide the year and give people equal amounts of time to recover from the last. This has been achieved by combining two cycles and standardising dates, which were probably never standard.

Our festivals have evolved from many sources, Celtic, Norse, Roman, even, dare I say it, Christianity.

Once people have become accustomed to seeing the modern cycle recorded frequently, it comes as something of a shock when a different pattern is given by someone else. (With different spellings too!)

In *West Country Wicca*, Rhiannon Ryall gives us only five festivals.

"The five festivals they did celebrate were as follows:

25th March Lady Day
30th April Beltane
21st June Summer Solstice
31st October Samhain
21st December Winter Solstice"

In *"Earth Magic"* by Margaret McArthur you will find the following list, Yule (or Winter Solstice), Beltane, Midsummer, Lughnassadh (or Lammas) and Samhain. Different again!

In *"Seasonal Magic - A Witches Guide"* by Paddy Slade, we have yet another pattern:

Samhain 31st October
Winter Solstice 21st or 22nd December
Imbolc 2nd February
The Vernal Equinox 21st-22nd March
Beltaine or May Eve 30th April
Summer Solstice &Midsummer Day 21st & 24th June
Lammas-Lughnasadh 1st-2nd August
The Autumnal Equinox 22nd-23rd September
Michaelmas 29th September

Of course, you might feel that they are just doing it to be difficult! Or different! My imagination gets loose again! Perhaps if you want to convince people that you are really traditional and are offering something truly original, then it is necessary to change the modern pattern! Leave some of the festivals out and so that people really get their money's worth, add a few new ones!

The main thing, is to try not to agree with any other books on the subject. This will at least keep everyone off balance and guessing. If you can get several festivals in quick succession, so that everyone becomes exhausted trying to keep up, so much the better!

There is an alternative theory. The Craft was never an organized religion with a central authority. If you look at the history of the Christian Church in this country alone, you will find some very major disagreements over such things as the date of Easter!

There are still Craft members who celebrate the festivals on different days to the dates commonly given now. Samhain, for instance, is celebrated by some on 13th of November. What they are intending to do is allow for changes that have taken place in the calendar.

Some celebrations may well have been held on the nearest full moon and certain groups prefer to follow this pattern. Many others celebrate on the nearest Saturday night for the simple reason that members of their group travel a long way and they need to gather when they can have the next day off to recover and quite possibly stay the night too. Drink driving laws have their part to play in the organisation of the Craft these days!

Other local needs dictated when festivals were held. Rhiannon states that little magical work was done outdoors during the bad weather of winter and during the heat of harvest time, everyone was just too busy to stop!

Other local events would take place at different times of the year, some fairs would fall on the quarter days, but there could be other local special days too. Some of the regular fairs around the country, like the Michaelmas Fair in Newbury, are now just the time when a regular fairground with its roundabouts and dodgems arrives. In the past though, they would have been times of great trade and people could come a long way to buy and sell there, or perhaps look for work.

Some fairs go back a very long way indeed and there are theories that certain of the old simpler "hill forts" were not so much built for defence, but to surround the gathering area and keep the flocks in! These affairs would go on for days too, with people wandering in, matters rising to a head and then people drifting away.

The majority of Pagans still seem to operate under this system, which is why they are appalling time keepers! For some, arriving the right day is good and being at the right site too is amazing! They are not, in reality, a few hours or days late, but several centuries behind! In fact, I think it must be a Pagan saying, (To borrow a few words from one of the world's great teachers,) "Wherever two or three are gathered together in my name, someone will be late!"

Saints who are honoured locally, perhaps having local springs or wells named after them, would have special days in the year given to them. What is even more interesting is that many of them are thinly veiled "covers" for the old local deities.

You have a Goddess whose symbol is that of a goose and she is linked to a nearby sacred well? Easy, link her to a Christian Saint, real, or invented for the occasion and think up some, probably slightly absurd, story linking her with geese. The well can then be honoured in her name. When her special saint's day comes round, Lo and behold! That locality displays its own variants of festival and some oddly Pagan elements are mixed into the local church celebrations.

You may wish to create your own cycle of festivals! You would not be the first, including Christianity. Quite a few of our "traditional" customs are not as old as we think and even some of the "old" ones turn out only to exist because they were "revived" at some point. You could include local customs and special "saint's" days.

A certain amount of feeling for the changing seasons would help it to feel more comfortable. It can also feel very odd when festivals are borrowed totally from another culture especially where the weather is completely different. If it is your collection of special days though, I suppose you can choose what you want!

Mind you, it can drive you quite mad trying to research some of them. One year my lunar calendar, gave February 22nd as "Stone Dropping Day", but omitted to mention what it was. Several conversations took place over the following year and it was not until I bought the next year's calendar that I discovered it was a Scandinavian custom of dropping a stone through a hole in the ice. If the hole stays clear, then Spring has come, if it freezes over, then Winter still reigns. (Well, at least I was kind enough to tell you!)

The following year, the calendar contained the fascinating date of "Mothering Thursday". After that, I would not have been surprised at them announcing a lunar Christmas.

These calendars are another reason for Pagans always being late. They have months based on different systems from countries and historical periods gathered from all over. Therefore, whilst you are in the third quarter of Elk, your friends, with a different calender are currently on the fourth day of Ribena.

Should, by some strange chance, you all arrive on the same day, you are wearing a set of horns you got at a car boot sale and they have a bunch of blackcurrants! (Warning! Humour is very important in Paganism and may break out at any moment!)

Perhaps you could research some old games to play on the festivals? Favourites like apple bobbing at Hallowe'en are still popular. There are marvellous games you can discover too, with wonderful names, like "Dwyle Flunking".

I turned up to watch this game once and in the way of such things, ended up playing. People dance in a circle, whilst one person in the centre tries to throw a wet beer soaked rag at them from the end of a stick. When I did it, I hit the referee! I thought I should get extra points, but no, I had to pay the penalty of drinking a pint in ten seconds. If I failed, it was to go over my head. I never knew I could drink so fast! I committed the terrible sin of reaching the finals absolutely pristine, unmarked, not a spot of mud, drop of beer or damp patch on me. I certainly was not by the end of that round! Some poor person had to drive me home! (It was not so much the beer as the bucket of mud tipped over my head that caused the problem.) Of course, it may be that this game had been invented by the pub landlord, instead of being very ancient. It was fun though!

I am suggesting that you can have a certain amount of choice and fun in the way that you choose to celebrate the changing seasons in the year. There are certain times when the seasons change and these have always been celebrated, but apart from the longest day and longest night, which are rather static, others have changed through history and from group to group, as have the ways in which they were celebrated.

It is far more important to have a sensitivity for the time of
year and the seasonal feeling than to run through some set
rite at a particular time that has no deep resonance within
yourself. Some of these things have a habit of happening
NOW and five minutes later is not the same, but that is
another story.

Further reading:

"Angels And Goddesses" by Michael Howard
"Sacred Ring" by Michael Howard
"The Eightfold Year" by Prudence Jones

Correspondences

I am sorry, but I have real trouble with these. You pick a periwinkle on the second day after the New Moon following the Autumn Equinox, but only if it is a Tuesday. You do it balanced on the back of a billy goat and return to your magenta draped temple to perform the magic whilst wearing a particular shade of magenta pink. The seventeen candles are made with bees wax and carved in the shape of cavorting nymphs. Your magic should then work. I SHOULD JOLLY WELL HOPE SO AFTER THAT LOT!

Yes, I know the logic behind it. Certain days attract certain planetary influences, herbs have magical, in addition to medicinal, properties and the sap rises and falls in cycles through the year and with the moon cycles. Wearing certain colours will alter the aura and help create healing and spiritual changes. I do realise that you do not have to understand something for it to work. I just feel that sometimes, it goes over the top!

I feel that one should work in the simplest way possible, with what is to hand and what seems appropriate.

I mean, now really think about this, and be honest, did the old village wise woman really have an almanac posted to her regularly telling her which planet was consorting with which? Yes, she may have looked up and noticed, but if farmer Gile's cow was poorly now, she had to act.

I agree that she had probably gathered a good supply of the magical herbs in advance at the right time of year. That was good housekeeping. She did it in the same way that she preserved the autumn fruit. It was part of life.

There is so much that is borrowed from high magic. It is there to impress the mind. It is also there to distract it with toys, to keep it busy while the imagination works magic. We should work to get beyond the toys.

So you are going to learn about colour? Wonderful! (You may find a strong urge to throw out most of your clothes though!) Learn about herbs and plants. Learn! Learn! Please, do not buy a kit in which someone sells you a load of fancy bits and pieces to attract a fortune and any nearby sexy people into your bed.

People do not even agree on such simple matters as working with the phases of the moon. Many consider the full moon to be the time to work magic, others argue that this is a time when the tide is slack. They work with waxing and waning moons (waxing or growing for things you wish to increase and waning for things you wish to decrease). Many say you should not work in the dark of the moon and yet there are people who always have.

By all means, learn about herbs and their meanings and uses, but learn about THEM. Appreciate them. Take time to get to know them as well. Smell them and look at them and meditate with them. Yes, a book will help you to learn. We do not all have a dear little old lady down the road full of ancient wisdom. (If there is and she does know something, she might not be a sweet little old thing, but a cantankerous old biddy. Some of them were you know!)

Similarly with stones and crystals. By all means read books about them, but sit with them and work out your own feelings too. Be aware, that if your thoughts differ from the book, it does not mean you are stupid or wrong, just that you may feel something different. Try to resist collecting too many as well. I am not just talking about digging holes in the ground and causing environmental damage. Like pets, you should only have as many as you can really care for and work with.

Remember too that you can work just as effectively (and perhaps more so) with a stone from the garden, or a pebble from the beach, as with an amethyst wrested from a mine in another part of the world. There are special stones all around you, just look and feel. For instance flint is a crystal and very widespread in the UK.

I know that you do need some guidance. I have an awful problem in that I find it terribly hard to follow a recipe book. Jon has therefore been treated over the years to such unusual meals as tuna and bacon casserole, pheasant and apple curry and rhubarb and raspberry jelly. (The last one would have worked better if the rhubarb had been sweetened first. As it was, the play of expressions across his face was quite an entertainment!) He said that the only thing that would really have complemented it was anchovies! There have been many more mundane meals too, I hasten to add!

Making up your own magical mixtures, without any help at all, unless you are wonderfully intuitive, could be a bit risky.

"Well, there I was trying to cure my neighbour's wart and all of a sudden this archdemon popped up! The trouble was, he did not have a sense of humour."

I mention the 'sense of humour' because there is a belief in certain circles that a nasty or unwanted manifestation can be banished by laughter. Always? Really?

It does help to research, but I just hate following instructions, without knowing why. I want to know why everything is included, rather than being given a complicated mixture, without explanation.

Some of my feelings stem from the fact that not all information is correct. For instance, Culpepper is known for recording herbal remedies. Some of them were collected from folk usage and had been tried for many years. Others though, had rather more dubious origins.

If a plant had a part that looked like a part of the body or seemed to link to a feature associated with a particular planet and therefore corresponded to a certain part of the body in the system being used, then it must cure it! (!) This is why you need a modern annotated version of *Culpepper's "Herbal"*, or another modern book, if you are to avoid making some serious and potentially dangerous mistakes.

Similarly, things within the Craft are handed down and the reasons for doing them become lost in time. They become simply a superstitious act, mixed in with what is really needed.

I guess what I am discussing is the difference between painting by numbers and learning to paint what you see and how you see it.

The thing to work on, is yourself. Give yourself time and understanding. Give yourself love and information. Work with what is simple.

There are many good books around which can help. More than books though, you need to follow your own feelings. If something feels right to you, then by all means explore its use in incense and on the altar. If another herb is deemed correct, but you do not like it, trust your reaction and seek another.

I hasten to add, that you must apply commonsense to this. Do not start dosing yourself, or worse still, others with herbal mixtures which simply feel nice to you. If you wish to learn about herbalism, do so very slowly and carefully. Start with very simple remedies like mint and camomile.

I must admit that someone who has just read their first book on herbalism and sets about brewing for the world, does fill me with a certain amount of terror. Be very cautious of what you accept from other people too. Jon knows a woman who made another person unconscious for 24 hours with a "cold cure" which involved rather too much poppy. It could have been worse.

I must admit to a hatred of "kits" for spells which can be purchased. I guess people take time and trouble putting them together. They may save the user time from gathering unlikely things and maybe they work? But this ignores the fact that collecting is part of the act of concentrating on the magic and most sensible magical aims which are going to be achieved anyway, may be achieved without the aid of complicated materials.

There are many truths flying about for the learning in the current age. One of them is NOT:

"If it costs a lot, is complicated and I cannot make head nor tail of understanding it, it must be good."

The above seems so prevalent as a "truth" within the commercial "aids" such as magazines, that it is putting many people off gaining from the terrific rush of energy and opportunity for spiritual growth that really is flowing out there, far beyond the sham and the money.

Which reminds me, I have something else to do...

Surfs Up! Let's go surfing!

Incense

Incense not only adds a great deal to a rite, it is also great fun to make! I have to admit that most of my earlier efforts tended to smell rather like a smouldering compost heap. I have more success now, because I use more of the resins and oils in mixtures.

Some of the older recipes used just herbs. After all, the local wise woman was unlikely to have frankincense about the house. They do not seem to burn as well or as long, but years ago, that was what people had available. There were native resins available though, using native trees such as pine and birch.

I have an attitude to cooking which means that it is almost impossible for me to follow a recipe exactly as it is written. This makes for interesting eating and sometimes even the chickens are not too sure about the results!

Similarly, I like to experiment with incense ingredients. It is great fun to see what there is and invent combinations. There should always be a degree of spontaneity about it. Having said that though, certain herbs and resins do have particular effects, in the same way that a herbal tea or inhaling aromatherapy oils will help to ease an illness if chosen well. Therefore, although it is fun to experiment and to create different mixtures, their medical and magical properties need to be studied also.

What is needed to start mixing your own? You can spend a lot of money, but savings can be made at first.

A pestle and mortar (or a container and an old knife or spoon?) A bowl to place the burning incense upon, (or an upturned empty tin on a saucer?) Charcoal blocks, Herbs, Resins, Oils, Matches (do not forget the matches on your five mile hike to the "Lurching Lepers".)

Charcoal Blocks

Charcoal blocks, like spark plugs, need to be kept dry, otherwise they can be <u>very</u> hard to light. Keep them in the airing cupboard or put them on the boiler for a while before use. They should light with a match or lighter, but I often seem to end up holding them in the flames of the open fire with the firetongs. The most over the top attempt to light one that I have seen involved a blow torch! (I have heard of another involving summoning a fire elemental and many holes burnt in the carpet, but the lady who told me wants to put the story in her book, understandably, so I will say no more.)

Herbs

Dried herbs can be obtained cheaply by growing them. Many dried kitchen herbs and spices can be used too. It is possible to find some in the wild, but remember that there are laws protecting many wild plants nowadays.

Do not be a vandal. Even things like Christmas mistletoe can be kept and dried. (In some parts of the country, it was kept in the house until the following Christmas anyway.)

Remember that many plants are poisonous and some of them can make their presence particularly felt when they are burnt and inhaled. Be cautious. Some herbs, for instance, mugwort, can be very potent indeed. Remember, you are not just creating a pretty smell! They can also be bought, but this almost feels like cheating! Some things though, such as most resins, just have to be purchased.

Resins

These keep the mixture burning and also offer something very special. Herbs on their own tend to be disappointing, but you can burn resins alone.

Pine resin might be obtainable in this country. Use beads that have already oozed out of the tree. Do not go round damaging trees. As anyone who has dealt with unseasoned pine knows though, be prepared for it to be very sticky! Pine

needles can also be used. You will normally expect to buy
other resins. They tend not to be cheap, but you need only
small amounts.

Pine

The scent of pine is linked with healing energies, also with
protection and for purification. It is especially applicable
during the winter months.

Dragon's Blood

Although called blood, this red substance is a plant resin. It
will repel malevolent psychic forces and attract good ones.
It is good to use when a house needs to be cleansed and
then the windows should be opened to allow the bad
influences to leave. Afterwards, a positive incense such as
frankincense should be burned.

Frankincense

I find the scent of frankincense exquisite and was lucky
enough to be given a box of it which came from Oman.
Frankincense will raise the level of vibrations and is
spiritually elevating. It is the major constituent of church
incense. I find it often helps if an atmosphere is troubled.

Benzoin

Benzoin attracts the higher spiritual forces and brings them
closer to us. It is used in some church incenses. Used with

frankincense, the effects of both are increased. It can sometimes be bought in chemist shops.

Myrrh

Myrrh is also found in many church incenses. Myrrh attracts the astral realms, helping to form a doorway and makes movement between levels easier. As such, it should be used with caution and only in conjunction with an elevating incense like frankincense. Before I knew that, I tried burning it alone, but it did not feel very satisfactory.

Oils

A very few drops of oil will improve the mixture. Now can be a good time to add an essential oil, but be careful as it can swamp the mixture with too strong a scent. It can also drown your dry ingredients if you put too much in. If you use another base or vegetable oil to dilute it, experiment first, some give off an annoying "fat" smell which can ruin your work.

I love frankincense and as an essential oil, I use it undiluted as a perfume, but be careful if you try this, some people have too sensitive a skin to use it in this way. It can be diluted with another oil though, such as almond oil and it is good for skin, especially the more mature skin!

This mixture makes a lovely oil to use for annointing during rites and it goes a lot further when diluted! It can vary greatly in price and recently I was given a bottle which was only half full, whereas in another shop, the bottle cost less and it contained twice the amount. They may vary in quality too though, you will have to decide your own favourites!

Always remember that these ingredients have both magical and medicinal results. If you burn them with others present, you are especially responsible. If you have pregnant women around, be <u>very</u> cautious indeed. Some essential oils are dangerous and should not be used when pregnant women are present, for example, fennel, rosemary, basil, marjoram, cypress, clary sage, juniper, pennyroyal, myrrh.

There are gentle ingredients such as lavender, and personally, I would still use frankincense myself and have read that it is considered safe to use during pregnancy, but you really need to look very carefully at what you are mixing and ask if it might not be better to stop experimenting for a while if you are not absolutely certain that your ingredients are totally safe. Some sources suggest that even lavender should not be used in the first six months of pregnancy where there is a reason to fear a chance of miscarriage.

A mother-to-be needs to be directing her energies inside herself anyway at that very magical time. She may like some restful fragrances to help her relax and meditate upon her child, but a great many other activities are not really for her when her energies are so importantly engaged.

I will give a very simple recipe though, should a pregnant lady wish to mix some incense. It consists of:

    Frankincense resin
    Lavender stalks and flowers
    Lavender essential oil

This will produce a very gentle "high vibration" incense suitable for a mother to meditate and think calm and spiritual thoughts about and possibly, to, her baby. It should also be very relaxing.

Mixing

Grind your dry ingredients with the pestle and mortar. Decant into a non absorbent container to add a few drops of oil. Place small amounts on the burning charcoal and store any left in a sealed container.

I am not going to give you a list of recipes. It is far more fun to discover your own, but I will share just one. This was a "what is in the house, what seems right" mixture for Samhain, made especially after someone had phoned up and upset me, so I needed cheering up too. I did not look up the meaning of the ingredients until afterwards. It smelled wonderful.

Samhain Incense

Herbs

Mostly Mugwort with pinches of, lavender, tansy, rosemary, and scented geranium leaf

Resins

Frankincense and myrrh

Oil

Benzoin essential oil

The mugwort gave off a scent which would have attracted all the local bobbies but they would have been most disappointed if it was tested in a laboratory for illegal substances! The incenses and oils added a strong, sweet background fragrance. It is a good idea to make a note of your ingredients, it can be impossible to remember later.

However, I urge you to be a little cautious about the "lucky dip" approach to incense making before a major rite which you have a specific result in mind for. Until you have an intuitive feeling for your ingredients it is probably best to experiment first!

Use tiny amounts when experimenting. (I mean like parts of a teaspoon full, or even using the end of the handle for resins such as Dragon's Blood which is not cheap. Keep an old spoon just for this.) You need very little and some ingredients can be expensive. It can be frustrating if you have just created a large amount of an incense mixture which really does not appeal to you!

Attributes Of Ingredients

The attributes of these ingredients are as follows,

Mugwort   enhances psychic vision,
                                 protective, healing

Lavender	love, protection, purification, happiness, to see ghosts (!)
Tansy	health and longevity
Rosemary	remembrance, happiness, childish openness
Scented Geranium Leaf	protection
Myrrh	brings other worlds nearer
Frankincense	raises vibrations, spiritually elevating
Benzoin	directly attracts higher spiritual vibrations

I leave you to think of some of your own mixtures and have fun!

Should you wish for further information and sample recipes however, the following books may be of help.

Further reading and bibliography

"A Handbook Of Psychic Protection" by Draja Mickaharic
"Magical Aromatherapy" by Scott Cunningham
"Cunningham's Encyclopedia of Magical Herbs" by Scott Cunningham
"Earth Magic, A Seasonal Guide" by Margaret Mcarthur
"Earth Dance - A Year Of Pagan Rituals" by Jan Brodie
"Magical Incenses And Perfumes" by Jan Brodie
"Psychic Self Defence - Real Solutions" by Jan Brodie
"Witches Of Oz" by Julia and Matthew Philips

Addresses for ingredients,

Neal's Yard Remedies, 14, Covent Garden, London, WC2. Also branches in, Oxford, Bristol, Brighton, Norwich and Bromley.

Starchild, The Courtyard, Glastonbury.

Life's Little Wisdoms

Unfortunately, the following gems are the result of people discovering these matters the hard way.

1. Never pick up a lit metal incense burner with your bare hands. They conduct heat astonishingly well!

2. Do not strew your circle with cat mint if there are likely to be cats in the vicinity. The devastation that one or more ecstatic cats can wreak on a circle has to be seen to be believed!

3. If you bury crystals in the earth to cleanse them, mark them very, very clearly. Small plant markers do not work as they will be removed by children, birds, cats and people digging who do not notice them at the time. When you come to dig the stones up, accept that they may well have moved anyway, (How do you think all those stones appear on the surface of your nice smooth seed bed?) Use something like a child's plastic spade to dig them up, not a metal garden spade, unless you want a pile of crystal shards when you finish. When you really cannot find it, accept that maybe it was not meant to be and perhaps it has a job to do in the earth and when you have finished explaining this to everyone else, go away somewhere private, on your own and curse loudly!

4. I know that incense sticks are frowned upon by many who feel that you should mix your own, even if it does smell like the compost heap caught fire, but these do have advantages sometimes. In addition to the fact that they are easy, should you be working in the dark, especially outdoors, you can wave them around like sparklers and so add that little extra something when you draw circles, sigils, pentagrams, your initials or whatever else you are into drawing! If working outdoors, seek to add insect repelling ingredients to your incense.

5. Never say, "Well, at least it is not snowing." A friend did and I think barely a minute passed before the blizzard struck.

6. Never associate the words "picnic" or "barbecue" with any magical event that you wish to be held outdoors. You will be lucky if it simply rains.

7. Do not ever plant tansy directly into your garden. It spreads by root and by seed and if it could only type would probably spread using the Internet too. That word, "invasive" was invented especially for this weed, sorry, useful herb.

I know people who unwillingly have a tansy lawn, which they have to mow. Cute you think? After all, one can have camomile and thyme lawns? Yes, but tansy grows up to six feet tall and develops woody stems. Do not give it to your friends without warning them to keep it in a pot and lift it regularly to trim the roots or it will burst the pot eventually and warn them to dead head it, (cut off the dead flowers) before it seeds everywhere. Perhaps I grew an especially vigorous strain, but friends have had to move house to escape it! Oregano and feverfew will cover a whole garden in a couple of years too!

8. I watched this one from the sidelines. The Pagan world does not need enemies. They can do far more damage to themselves. Do not ever write "for the eyes of initiates only" or similar on a document unless you want it photocopied, handed out to all and sundry and even entered on the Internet!

9. Do not (and this one is serious) allow someone involved in magic into your home if you do not know and trust them and certainly, never work magically or open yourself up psychically with a person you feel uneasy with or in a situation which gives you a niggling feeling that all is not well. Truly, it can take years to sort out the mess.

10. By all means, listen to other's advice and warnings, but do not take them for the unarguable truth, including what I say.

Little Everyday Acts of Magic Whilst Driving

I am not thinking here of driving along in your car and summoning up a great being from another plane with a complicated set of rituals. That, assuming you were driving, would be a very good way to enter a new state of awareness in a rapid and somewhat permanent manner!

A friend of mine had someone who decided to meditate whilst driving to his meditation class. Unfortunately, they rather damaged the entrance to his drive on arrival!

There are many psychic acts which can take place whilst driving however. You can exercise your will in trying to get people to pull into the inside lane so that you can overtake them. This is not quite the same as imagining that you have a James Bond car and can blast them out of your way! If all their wheels drop off, you will be left with a question of how much "And it harm none" was functioning at the time and a nasty mess in the road to avoid.

This gives you some idea of how many failsafe devices the human brain has on it to stop such thoughts causing instant effects in the world. If they did not exist, most of our roads would be one big scrap heap.

I heard one young man describe how he had wished that an annoying woman would fall down and had been shocked and felt guilty when the person next to her had done so. Chance?

There are those who are always good at finding parking spaces. It is possible to switch on the belief that a space will be available as you approach the spot. This often works for me, except one time when my dentist called me in for an appointment at short notice when I had other things to do. I had to park a long way away and Jon said that was because I did not want to go!

It can be a good idea to put up psychic protection whilst driving. Do not, however, lose concentration on what you are doing! Try it as a passenger at first perhaps. One person commented that they visualised a wonderful sphere of light about their vehicle before driving off. They drove away and the protective bubble stayed where the vehicle was parked! It was quite tricky for them to think of it as moving along!

Think of the protection as being around the vehicle, like bumpers on a dodgem if you like, rather than associating it with the space where it is standing.

I was given quite a strong warning about a near accident recently. I was entering a car park on a sunny day, when I felt a strong sensation as if the car had been hit from the right hand side. There was the shock of impact and the sensation of crushing metal and noise. Having had no car accident experiences for a long time, (touch wood) and having never been in an accident where the impact came on the driver's door, I was surprised. I thought, "It is a sunny day, people do stupid things on sunny days, be careful". About half an hour later, as I was driving the short distance home, a car on the other side of the road decided to turn off and travel down the road to my left and swung straight across without warning. I was just able to avoid collision, ending up on a grass verge. The driver, (an elderly man) then turned round in a one way slip road and drove back out from it! The people in nine vehicles sat watching in fascination, not daring to move in case he headed for them next! I am very thankful for the warning.

There are drivers who are also very good at avoiding traffic jams, often choosing an alternative route for no logical reason, only to hear later that the road was blocked. Perhaps in addition to radio broadcasts, they should have telepathic traffic news?

Jon also has an amazing ability to find a destination that he has never been to before. He will dive off down a side street, turn right, turn left and be right outside the correct building! I am able to lose a place I have visited a dozen times. At a folk festival years ago, I arrived at a different place nearly every night and almost never the one I aimed for! I thoroughly enjoyed wherever I found myself though. Like Pooh and Piglet, when they were lost, sometimes the only way to find somewhere is to stop trying to get there! Then, if you end up somewhere else anyway, perhaps that is where you were meant to be!

I can find places (or lost objects), by one of two methods. The first involves precise instructions which are followed logically. The second, usually safer on foot, involves giving up conscious control and following instincts. Unfortunately, combining the two, up to now, has left me very lost on occasions! The logical brain starts to argue with the intuitive brain and it all falls apart. This is what is happening all the time in our lives. We have to switch that side of our brain off which says, "It cannot be!" to anything unusual.

There are those who find that driving creates a relaxed frame of mind in which intuitive thoughts are able to come to the fore. The important thing again, is not to get too relaxed. There is a difference between a straight piece of local country road and the Talgarth Roundabout in London. (If you are not driving, when negotiating this traffic nightmare, I advise you to keep your eyes shut and if you are driving, it may help as I suspect from the way all the other vehicles are swinging around, the other drivers are refusing to look too!)

I know that other people in addition to myself have often had warnings about an animal or child about to run across the road. I remember seeing a group of children on a pavement and hitting the brakes a few vital split seconds before one child swung away from the group, straight into the road in front of me. You still need to use all your logical faculties too though, as sadly, intuition is not always enough.

One place which has given several people a surprise recently is Twyford Down near Winchester, site of that infamous new piece of road which has devastated a once beautiful area. When we were about to drive through the deep cut in the ancient hill, there was a terrific shock. It was as if the hill still felt itself to be there. Currents of energy ran right across the road from one half of the hill to the other. There was a feeling of unreality and the vehicle in front seemed to look like a computer game or even, not there. It was extremely dangerous. There are sensitive people who have awful headaches and feelings of pressure at this point. I contacted Dragon, the environmental group and it seems that others have had similar experiences, there have also been a number of accidents there already.

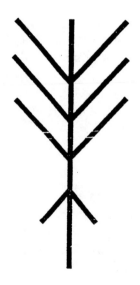

The Dragon Rune

Jon and I tried different ways of dealing with the problem. I tried to form a protective bubble around us, or to imagine a tunnel through the energies, but this did not work well. Jon thought of the energies as passing through him. What I found worked best and others have since tried and agreed, is to think thoughts of healing and love. It did not seem so bad the last time we drove through, so there must be quite a few people who are sending out their healing thoughts. So many people fought so hard to try and save the site that a strong psychic mark had been left there by the combination of their energies and magic and the Earth energies of the place.

People are realising the madness that has been going on with the road building and the destruction of ancient sites and those of natural interest. It has been so great that it has almost seemed that there was a campaign to destroy worthwhile things, perhaps before people demand that such spots are truly protected in future, rather than seen as a cheap position for yet another monstrosity which will make money for a few people and destroy a site of value to all for ever.

So often have roads been planned over these irreplaceable sites in recent years, that one wonders if cost is really the only reason behind the orgy of destruction.

Sometimes I imagine a planner, drawing all the ancient and beautiful and rare places on a map and then drawing a great wiggling and curving line so that it passes through as many as possible. They can always add an extra giant roundabout or two, to develop later, should one or two be missed.

It was bad enough when the Romans did it, but at least the Romans just built in straight lines!

Housework Magic

Many people have written on the aids and ingredients which may help with magic.There is crystal magic,for instance and the use of flowers, herbs, trees, water, even animals.

Nowhere however, have I seen an article on the use of housework magic.

It is all very poetic, crossing a starlit moor, three days after the new moon to pick a dandelion at Midnight, but when you have to catch the 6.30 to Paddington next morning, it has disadvantages.

Housework magic is for the busy person. How many times have you been unable to fulfil a psychic need because you just do not have the time to polish the seventeen branch candlestick before you even start? Think of how much time you could save if the magic was completed while you polish!

Here is an example. A heavy, unwanted influence is settling on your life. Get out your polishing materials, using tissues or unwanted rag. Polish away, thinking of all the black marks being removed as the unwanted influence. When you finish, dispose of the rags and wash your hands thoroughly.

Life has become dull and dingy? Give the windows a good clean and concentrate on all the light pouring into your life.

Open the curtains wide in the morning and let the sun rush in! Open the window and let in fresh air to blow away any stale negative vibrations hanging about!

Scrub the walls and floor and as the black water flows down the drain, think of all the bad things leaving your life.

Tidy the books, magazines, toys, shoes, magic wands, plastic goat skulls etc. away and think how organised your life is becoming.

Your guests became a bit heavy when they stayed? Put a pinch of salt in the washing machine when you wash the guest bedding and towels. (Just a pinch, you do not want to ruin the machine!)

There is a personal link that needs breaking? Get some scissors and top and tail the beans, thinking of the link, not the person, however annoying they might be!

Get a huge feather duster and flick the dust off everything- and - just enjoy it! The cat will love it! You can vacuum the mess up, including the remaining feathers, empty the bag and Hey Presto! More Magic!

Now that the house is clean and tidy, you might fancy setting up a few candles, thinking up a circle and- maybe- just relaxing with some cakes and wine!

After you have finished laughing, I will warn you that in the right frame of mind, it works! You really do not need all the paraphernalia to push things from the physical world into the next, they are closer than you think!

Found Magic

Do you remember when you were a little child and you went for a walk in the country or on a beach and you came back with your pockets stuffed full of treasures? There were feathers and acorns and conkers and pebbles which looked like jewels until they dried. There were seashells and seaweed that popped and hazelnuts and twigs and discarded eggshells. A whole world of fascinating, colourful objects returned home with you and your mum tried to lose some of them over the next few weeks, especially the smelly seaweed and the bone that you thought was probably a fossil.

I still do it! I find that the simplest natural things have a fascination far beyond so much that is manmade. I return with feathers and odd ears of corn from stray plants blown into the hedgerows. (It is not reasonable to wade into a farmer's crop, trampling all underfoot to help yourself.) I find the most wonderful feathers and pick up smooth pebbles. Occasionally, I ask a tree if I may take a twig or two home to remind me of the season. Hazel catkins remind me of spring outside and drop pollen everywhere and a few holly berries welcome Yule into the home.

With the recent fashion for North American Indian matters and for Shamanism, the making of medicine objects or fetishes is becoming more common. A feather and a few twists of wool may become a reminder of a special walk or a

100

gift to leave in a place which means a lot to you. Be careful what you leave though. Organic materials which will decay or be eaten by wild creatures can be a good idea. Foreign or manmade materials could just become another form of litter. Many garden plants are poisonous and should not be left near livestock. You must think carefully.

A lot of magic is about being as simple as a child, but we have to add adult responsibility to that. We have to be careful of what we take nowadays. Crops belong to someone, as do woods. Many species are protected by law. As a child, I remember picking bunches of primroses, with friends, that all put together measured two feet across. We found them high up on the railway embankment, but then the banks were sprayed with weed killer and all the plants were gone. Although not all species are protected, we have to realise that we cannot just help ourselves today as in those happy, uncaring ways. It is all too precious. If we want our children to see these things, we have to leave them to grow and seed.

Try buying seeds and growing your favourite wild flowers in the garden instead. You might even like to grow your own corn, in a pot on the windowsill if you do not have a garden. You can often find grains of wheat in animal food mixtures in pet shops. It could be quite fun to cut your own corn at Lughnassadh!

Often, you do not need to remove anything living. Trees drop all sorts of wonderful things and even in town you can find parks where tall trees will drop seeds and leaves and twigs snapped in the wind. You can find wildlife too in the most urban settings.

I remember a city street in which there was just one wild buddleia bush pushing up through a crack to represent the green world and clinging to it was a host of chattering sparrows. What were they saying? They may have been praising the wonderful day, or they may have been shouting, "****** off! This is MY bush!"

What can you do with these things? You could learn some of the attributes of different trees and save parts of a relevant tree to use in a charm. You might place some tiny ash twigs over your door, for protection for instance, should you feel the need. There are many old charms recorded using natural things.

Do you sometimes get a walnut shell that breaks cleanly into two halves? Do you just throw it away without thinking, or are you childish like me and keep it and keep playing with it? You could seal a little healing charm in it or perhaps a favourite stone.

When I went to Avebury once, at a difficult time in my life, I brushed past an elder tree and a tiny piece of twig snapped off. I thanked the Lady for the gift and placed it in my pocket. I have often felt that little twig in my pocket since and felt reassured.

Again, you must be careful and thoughtful. We do not want trees stripped bare at the sacred sites as everyone rips bits off for their magic! Sometimes a tiny pebble or a feather may have a special meaning though when it comes in a sacred place or at a certain time in your life. Did you know that one owner of Stonehenge used to rent out hammers so that visitors could chip bits off the stones? Nowadays we are far more sophisticated. We put barbed wire and fences around some sites and build motorways over the rest.

You have to accept that your house will fill with a clutter of unimportant things, many of which will be of no use whatsoever. Unless you are very good at remembering, create a catalogue or can recall with psychometry, you will probably forget where half of it came from too! Never mind! At the very least it will make your house look as though you are really into natural magic. People will be intrigued, wondering what spells you are working, or, most likely, they may think what a child you are and that most of your home looks like something is nesting in it!

There is a belief that magic works better if you spend enormous amounts of money and buy expensive kits that someone else has put together. Then there is the belief that magic does not need to cost more than effort and love.

I will give an example. I wished to increase the protection around my home. Without consciously thinking about it, I placed blue glass bottles on windowsills, where they would catch the light. Why spend a fortune on a vase, when we have just the same beauty in something that we throw away? Most of them were moved when they were needed for our wine making. I put a blue vase on another windowsill, because it seemed a good place to tuck it out of the way.

Then I found an old peacock feather when tidying up. That seemed right displayed on another windowsill. I found a blue jay's feather which I brought home and our bantam cockerel moulted his feathers with a blue sheen. I made an arrangement of them and put them on a windowsill. I began to notice a pattern. The final touch was a bantam feather which the wind blew all around the house to catch in a cobweb by the front door, where it stayed for days, if not weeks.

The house was now surrounded by shiny blue, reflecting trouble outwards and encouraging those things associated with this higher colour, raising the spiritual vibration, one might say. I also had some pretty decorations on the windowsill, some simple feathers. I had not spent any money, just used what came to hand. It was a found magic, not only because I used found objects, but because my conscious mind had not even been aware of what I was doing. I only found out afterwards!

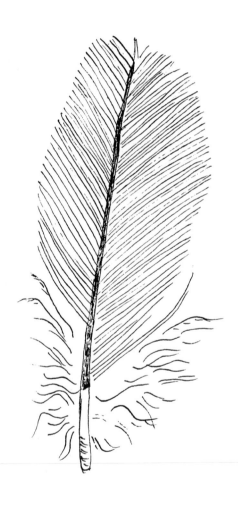

Working

Recently a journalist who had been looking for some Pagans to interview contacted us. He said that he wanted to hear what Paganism is really about and to discuss it with people who bring it into their everyday lives. I believe he really wanted to put forward a fair point of view. We spoke on the telephone. As the conversation went on, it turned out that photos were wanted. Could people be watched "working" and some of the words recorded?

I attempted to explain, that a lot of the magical work we do, consists of one or two people sitting very still and relaxed for a period of time. It can be great fun to raise power by dancing around, but sometimes power can simply be raised and sent without showing outward signs to people. I think this was very disappointing for him. Not only is it unexciting and not very photogenic, but since he has experience with the Quaker form of worship, it is remarkably similar to what he knows already.

It grows "worse", for it turns out that this gentleman had contacted many genuine people in the Pagan world, asking for the genuine thing and being told what it was. When he asked for the robes and the wacking great knives and the fancy words, he kept getting quiet sincere people who said, 'but that is not what we do'. He wanted the "real thing" but had already decided what that was. There grew a horrible fear that he would get one of the usual lens-loving people to wave an enormous kitchen knife about and say something facetious in appalling rhyme and will doubtless believe himself to be discovering the truth at last. (From what I heard, he eventually found a Gardnerian, who is fortunately quite widely respected and gave him his atmospheric photograph too.)

The fact is, that to an audience, unless they have psychic vision, nothing is happening so much of the time. Sometimes, there is a sound, that of gentle snoring, where someone has dropped off. Of course, if you are tired, then that is probably what your body needed anyway. It is not necessarily a failure though, for believe it or not, sleep can sometimes be the level of consciousness that is required for a change to take place. The conscious mind may be blocking an idea which is placed instead in the sleeping mind, to be absorbed slowly. It is also possible to be awake and conscious with the thinking, even when the body is so relaxed that it is sleeping. It is possible to sit there listening to oneself snore!

The last bits of information are very useful to know. If you are accused of falling asleep during a rite, you only have to explain that you were in fact accessing a deeper level of consciousness! Do not do it too often in company though and try a few early nights, or they may get suspicious!

I tried to explain to the journalist an occasion when a group of us had "worked" spontaneously at a sacred site, West Kennet Long Barrow. Nothing had been planned or discussed, we were just visiting it, much like tourists with some deeper feeling thrown in. Then it went quiet and one person started to concentrate, others joined in, without speaking, opening up to the energies there. One person, physically present, was quite unaware and kept putting in little everyday comments completely at odds with what the others were feeling. I felt a great rush of energy that swept right up through me, cleansing a lot of junk out of the system and leaving a calm energy behind. I felt a lot of gratitude to the one who had opened the place up and allowed the rest of us to share. Anyone watching, would not have seen a thing.

On another occasion, a group of us worked at Wayland's Smithy. This was more noticeable to those around, for a group of us stood in a circle, holding hands. We were composed of a wide range in age, right down to a crawling baby, who sensibly got bored and wandered off to try and sample the wine goblet! (Luckily it was full of fruit juice.) Few words were spoken and those quietly and after some time, everyone stepped into the centre, raised their hands and brought them down.

Boring, isn't it! No dramatic hand waving, no Rupert Bear poetry and no naked virgins! Where is the fun in that? The reaction of the public was fascinating, perhaps altered by the fact that we were being filmed at the time. A small group tried a few comments, but became bored with being ignored and most others just tried very hard to pretend we were not there!

It is of course fun to have a circle with all the trimmings. For many, it is the way that they feel happiest working. That is their way. There is great enjoyment in putting on a seasonal play, it can mean a lot to both the actors and those watching and there you have a problem. What if there is no one to watch? What if there are simply not enough of you?

There may not even be enough of you to act out the play! It can be very hard work, having to play the Oak King and the Holly King simultaneously and to have to fight yourself and club yourself to death twice a year! It reminds me of someone in a "radio" play years back at school, who was unwittingly cast in two roles which came "face to face" in an argument. He ran from one side of the microphone to the other, shouting at himself! (Yes, alright, you can say that it is only different aspects of ourselves and of deity that we are portraying, etc. It is still tough on small groups and single workers!)

It does help the mind to have some simple actions to perform, some words to say sometimes. I guess it helps some people to get in the mood and to understand things better. But for me, a lot of it intrudes. Performing can have great psychological benefits, but it is not working. If I must remember words, then I cannot concentrate on "working". Although I have remembered lines for plays and to recite poetry over the years, my mind goes amazingly blank in a working situation and I am mainly filled, not with inspiration, but pure terror and stagefright! Once, as I mentioned before, in an Earth Healing Rite, my original lines, which had been cut again and again for me, had been reduced to "Hail and welcome" and "Hail and farewell." I stood there with my arms held wide welcoming air at the start of the ceremony, hoping everyone would think it was a dramatic pause, or I was still visualising the element. But Jon knew. He knew I had forgotten my line! I could feel the wind all about me though, I could feel it in my mind. I do not think I am alone.

Of course, there is another sort of stagefright, that when you do NOT have a script to follow, when the words are not written down and everyone is waiting! That is when the words have to come from the heart, from deep inside you and if they are not there, then you have to ask what are you attempting to do and why?

Sometimes, the "inspiration" is to hand over to another. This is not just "passing the buck", it may well be that another person has the words within them. They may care more, be more involved, or even less emotionally involved and therefore able to step back and give a more balanced approach.

For example, a group of us gathered to try and help someone deal with a prolonged psychic attack. It was a drawn out matter which had affected the lives of most of the experienced people there. The one who took charge, unconsciously, by saying, "Shall we take hands then?" was rather more outside of the situation. (Later, they were to wonder if they had intruded, but that was not the case. Their objectivity gave a balance.) Each person there was given their turn to say what was in their hearts. There were other, non physical presences. In psychic terms, there was an awful lot going on that night. A photographer would have been deeply disappointed. A group of people stood in a circle, said a few words that did not even rhyme and then at the end, believe it or not, bounced up and down laughing to dispel the tension!

Laughter in itself is magic too, of course. Not unkind laughter, but real rippling laughter which grows. It does roll back those dark shadows!

Pagan Living

What is Pagan living? It means that everything that one does in life is effected by one's religious views. In a Christian, it is the difference between someone who writes C. of E. on a form and expects the Church to be there for weddings and Christmas and perhaps even turns up on Sunday occasionally and someone who puts their whole life into a Christian perspective. In the same way, a Pagan may take part in ever-so-many exciting rites, but yet not really be living the religion.

There are many ways to live it too. There are those who wear outrageous clothes, embarrass their neighbours and family with loud protestations and talk about the Goddess in gushing terms whenever possible. Their actions in the rest of their lives, may tell another story.

Then there is the living which involves making a living. This becomes very tricky. There are many pitfalls and moral dilemmas to be faced. Many draw a distinction between the working of magic and the sideline issues, such as writing, making pottery images of the Goddess, artwork or publishing! If one brings the world of business too close to that of magical and spiritual matters, then they can react badly towards each other. It may work, if you can grow two heads! Otherwise, the constant worry about financial matters can eat away at the peace of mind needed to concentrate on healing and helping others. On the other hand, if things are flowing as they should, it all moves towards an integrated whole.

Say that you decided to charge for healing though? It can become a constant battleground of personal ethics. What if someone needs help and they cannot afford you? What if someone offers money and you are not really sure if you are doing the best thing for them, but you need the cash? There have been gifted psychic healers who have been given the gift, made large fortunes and then had the gift taken away. Some have then continued to practice for as long as they can afterwards, although they are not really helping any more. On the otherhand, if you are a gifted healer who can save lives, should you work for eight hours a day as a supermarket shelf filler?

People who "tell fortunes" often also learn tricks of the trade and can make educated guesses that often prove right and this can lead to the insidious loss of their real abilities. It is also very hard to say to someone, "I can sense absolutely nothing, I do not have a clue!" when they have just paid you! I have been in groups where others are all busy "feeling the vibes" and said, "I cannot feel anything". It takes quite a nerve! It must be even harder if they are about to demand their money back!

Personally, I feel that everyone has a right to make a living. If they are running a shop, then they need to run it in a way that brings in a fair income. Similarly, a craftsperson has a right to be paid for their work, whether physical or mental.

There are those who try to use the Pagan idea as a lever to get free or cheap things. Oddly enough, it seems to work along the lines of you giving the advantage to them and trying to make you feel guilty because you would like to be paid your expenses or for the books that you have had to pay for etc. Oddly enough, these people seem to be very concerned about money when it is going towards them!

This is not the same as people helping each other. There are many instances where favours and reciprocal arrangements are being fairly exchanged. The Jews have done this for centuries, Freemasons too are firmly believed to have done this in addition to all those funny handshakes! It seems to be linked with the term "networking" at present. Personally, I look forward to the time we find a better word. "Networking" reminds me rather too much of a form of legalised brainwashing and pyramid selling techniques based on conning others into the same unfortunate mistake you made earlier. You can see why I hate the term! But then, "helping each other" does not have quite the same swing to it!

Many feel that if we have been given psychic gifts, then we should be thankful for them. If gifts have been given freely to us, then we should give freely. This will help to keep them untainted. Others feel that they should spend as much time as possible using their gifts, which means earning a living with them. We do need to live somehow though, so our means of making money needs to be well handled, fairly, to ourselves as well as others. Each must decide for themselves what is Craft, what is a Pagan linked hobby and what is work. We can still apply our ethics to the business, but we must apply a little hard sense too! Eventually, of course, we must all decide for ourselves.

So what actually IS pagan living. Well, of course, it is so much easier to say what it is not. It seems to be a bit like riding a bike, succeeding or falling off are both easier than describing it!

There are not even huge lists of rules set out. Some groups have a few written rules and others do not go much further than "And it harm none." Those who imagine a vast church-like structure of accepted practices (and people!) are in for a hard time! Not only will no two groups agree, but rarely will two people be able to think the same and then only for a while!

You have to try and work out your own ethics and then realise that some will change and some will be impractical. Let me give you an example. I too wish to, well, if not save the planet, at least slow its destruction. So I used environmentally friendly washing powder. Perhaps it was my old machine, or the low temperature washes, or our hard water, but the washing just got greyer and greyer. Brand new things went in white and came out grey. Eventually, I went back to a powder that worked. It was not just that the clothes came out depressing and dowdy, it was not good psychically either as all that dirt clung to the clothes. So? That was a housework problem, it was a green problem, but it also was a matter of ethics and psychic good health.

One can claim to be Pagan and not care two hoots about the planet and anyone else, though there will be several lives worth of lesson learning to follow. One can care like mad and not be Pagan. What else makes one Pagan?

You basically come down to a view of the world, or, I should say worlds and the way in which they blend and interact. Here I will have to talk about my own views, for I cannot claim to make a statement that covers everyone else, assuming you could freeze them all in time right now! As the ancient Celts believed, this world and the other worlds all exist together and interlink. The world of spirit, the lower realms and the physical plane all exist and work together, constantly interacting. Actions, words and thoughts move between them and cause changes. A wish becomes real on another plane, causes changes and returns to Earth to cause changes here. That is magic. Those are miracles. That is life.

We are, as physical beings, but a part of ourselves and our waking selves are only a tiny part of our consciousness. Our physical life is but a tiny part of our eternal selves. This is wonderful! It is a really encouraging faith to have. Not only does one suddenly have a lot more time, but you get eternal life too!

Yes, I know other religions say these things too, but then surely humans have to get some things right and in agreement!

I believe in reincarnation, because it just does not seem possible to learn enough in one life time. In fact, many, world religions believe in it, as did Christians until it was made a heretical belief. I KNOW I cannot do and learn enough in one little life. I KNOW my body will wear out long before my thirst for knowledge would. I cannot believe that the developing soul would be wasted because a physical body could no longer sustain it.

I cannot envisage a deity who is representing just one human sex. It seems quite ludicrous to me! Ultimate deity must be without human ideas of individual gender. Since it is beyond the comprehension of our minds, either limited in life by our brains or outside of physical life by our level of understanding, then the majority of Pagans divide their view of deity into male and female, the Lord and the Lady. This seems fair.

I recently watched a wedding blessing ceremony conducted in an old church by a male priest and a robed lady helper. Whether she was ordained or not, I do not know. I just know that they radiated a feeling of love, harmony and balance that would be worthy of any religion worth its salt. The priest held out buttercups to the congregation that had been handed him by a small child. Yes, this was a Christian celebration. You see, all the best things come to an agreement!

I believe, that whilst being aware of our spiritual and eternal nature, we must admit our responsibility to the physical plane that we have manifested in. We must care for our bodies, those around us and for the things of this world. As we grow, our values change and you realise that emotions and love are worth far more than so many trivial things.

Now there are those who will be getting annoyed with this view. "Too New Age" they may say. (Like all terms that come and go, this one is beginning to become an insult.) Too much "White Light". (There is nothing wrong with white light, it is just the sentimental and commercial rubbish that survives under its banner that sticks in the throat.)

I cannot pretend to be a stone age shaman, or a Red Indian. I cannot claim to be a medieval witch, but recently toasted, doing odd things with goats bottoms. Even in those times, they did not agree with each other! I live in this century. In this life, I have these problems and these ethical possibilities to face and so have you. You may not have to decide whether to club your neighbour over the head in order to steal his kill, but you may feel like doing it when he will not turn his stereo down! A few centuries ago, you might ask, will I get to eat today? In our culture, in this country, most of us can ask instead, should I go vegetarian?

(Yes, I know far too many people really are short of food, whatever those who have far too much misused power and money would want us to believe.) For many of us, anyway, there is a choice.

Surely, being Pagan is about rituals and acts of magic? There are those who are Pagan without doing those. There are those who perform them, without really living the religion. There are those for whom it is a system to get what they want and not a religion at all.

What about making people do what you want? What about commanding elementals to do your bidding, forcing them against their will? And there you have it, morality again. (I do not mean whether your petticoat is showing.) Undoubtably there are those who have worked with the things of Earth and spirit to gain their own way, in the same way that the Victorians thought nothing of killing thousands of animals in a day for sport, or trying to be the one to kill the last of an almost extinct species. We still have fox hunting. We keep animals in batteries. It is a question of ethics, of caring. At a certain point, you decide not that you cannot do something, but that you should not.

You get very different ethical decisions to make than if you live in a drought-racked war zone or another century. You can think about the spiritual life at your leisure, instead of wondering how soon you and your sick starving children are going to enter it. And we see all this happening, on our televisions. It is thrown at us nightly, almost, it seems, more than the news of our own country. The cameras go up on our roads and all we see is distant wars. A huge road is built through our local nature reserve and the television shows us drought far away.

I feel that you have to work on that which you can reach, when you can reach it. Start with now, start with you and then your family and loved ones and work outwards. Unless you are one of those people who heads out to these disaster areas to help. Help your friends and neighbours and those who come into your life first. Do perhaps little, but real things and you will have gone some way to living your own religion.

There are those who talk about the "Golden Times" when everything was wonderful and some say women ruled the Earth and there was no war or famine or illness.... Humans have always dreamed of such times, either in the past, or to come. A million Utopias have been dreamed. The trouble is, the world is not like that, it is not meant to be. What people are dreaming about, or remembering, are the other worlds of our existence, where such things are possible.

Do not try and create myths about a religion which has remained the same through centuries as if it is a serious philosophy as times and values have changed. For some, maybe, it has not, but where is the progress in that?

Is Paganism not something very old? Something which we should try to preserve because of its very antiquity? There is a difference between keeping the knowledge of something and putting it to a use which we now know is wrong. It is very sad if old things of value are lost because of the coming of something new and at first glance more exciting, but it is worse to perpetuate that which we have developed beyond.

It is good to have tradition, but if it tries to stop it becomes at best a fossil, at worst that which promotes cruelty and lies to keep itself alive. Some of the most aware religious groups will even let themselves die out, seeing that a new religion carries the thrust of human spiritual development forward. I believe in the roots of tradition, but a tradition which changes.

The traditions varied and disagreed anyway and containing humans, they contained that which was commendable and that which was not. Drowning a young girl in a bog as a sacrifice to your deity may have seemed reasonable two thousand years ago, it is distinctly frowned upon in most circles now.

We are in a terrific time of change and are privileged to be here now, but, as with all privileges, something has to be given back, it is never easy. We who have chosen to stand with our feet on the Earth are now looking at the stars, it is quite a stretching experience! It seems to me that we have gone back to our roots to gather that which we felt was good. Sometimes we have picked up a fair bit of nonsense along the way too. This is partly our wish to be comfortable, our wish to stop, our wish to "come home." One does not stop though, for coming home is but a time of rest, a time of recognition, the realisation that you have placed your feet upon the right path. So, when you have travelled to the beginning, you take what you have learned and you move back onto your path again.

There can be a feeling that if we go back far enough, we will find the thing which is ultimately right and some people do find things which they choose to stay with. But, others of us are restless and we get out the sandals and the staff and we are off again.

You have to be careful with this though, firstly to respect the knowledge and the people that give it to you along the way and secondly to be careful not to throw the baby out with the bathwater. Sometimes, I think people have kept the bathwater! When there are fancy words and complicated rituals, it can be possible, for a time, to be bedazzled and think you have arrived. You have never arrived, you may have simply stopped for a while. After a time, the questions will begin to filter in and you will start to get restless and the feet get itchy and those sandals come out again.

I have found that often in life, one gets pushed into the next change, frequently shouting and screaming. The job becomes unbearable, the neighbours become impossible, the lease runs out. For some, the push is very hard, illness, bankruptcy, prison. So it can be with religious ideas.

Have you ever had that desire to completely change your wardrobe? To throw out nearly everything in it and start again. I have. Being a natural hoarder, I manage to throw away very little and often regret the little I did! I truly admire people who can pare down the things in their lives to the bare essentials. It is wonderful to clear the clutter, but sometimes you lose an item of value too.

In some ways, the development of the Craft is the same. There are the old and dear things, there are the clothes discovered in the antique shops, made with marvellous materials, but a wardrobe of clothes is not a museum piece. Neither is it a dressing up box.

I think that the Craft has to take a great step, it is changing, it is growing up and moving on. There will be people who stop and hold their positions all along the way, but unless it dies, some will always be moving on. Eventually, it will change so much, that it will be called something different, with its roots in the Craft. (I do not mean here new fashions which have simply found a new name for something old.)

And here is the strange thing, because in moving on, it will come round in a circle again, back to where it was, but a little further on. Do you see what I mean? It is that spiral again! In the same way one can move around a circle, building the power, so understanding is also built up. So, one returns again and again to the source of inspiration, gaining more understanding each time around.

It seems that much of modern Wicca has lost its spirituality and yet that is what it is straining towards. Hundreds and thousands of years ago, people lived in a world permeated by spirit. In both looking back and looking forward, we are seeking the same thing.

We are seeking to reconcile the physical world and spirit, the Earth and the Sky, just as we have always done. Earth below and Sky above. It is in that tension between the two that we learn and develop. As with the active and passive principle, the instrument of fertilisation and that which is made fertile, Male and Female, it is within that tension, that both the religion and our own development remains alive.

Thirteen things to help your development

Thirteen! Now there is a wonderful number! There are thirteen moon months in the year. If I was very clever, I would give you something to do each month, but you will simply have to organise it as you see and feel best! Some things may not appeal to you at all and others you may not feel like doing for years. All people are different and therefore learn in different ways and at different rates.

1. Learn To Meditate

To many people, this means sitting somewhere in an excruciatingly painful position, muttering "OM". It does not have to be done this way, indeed, I find the position impossible, except as a form of self torture, which I do not feel has a great deal to do with my spiritual development. I once heard an Eastern teacher explain that he made his pupils sit for several hours in that position, willing themselves to overcome the pain. I am probably one of those lily livered people who would have looked for another teacher! This may not do so much for my psychic will power, but it will do wonders for my back and hip joints!

Find a comfortable position. If it is so comfortable that you fall asleep, either change it, or admit that your body is trying to tell you something and have a few early nights! It is possible to be partly awake, so that you can hear yourself snoring, (should you be prone to it!).

It is also possible for your brain to "split" into two, so that one half goes warbling on about the gas bill and what to cook for dinner and the other half is strangely free to think on higher things. This can be useful if the "everyday" half can keep a watch out for the baby crying, or if you are working with others, consider how they are feeling, whether they want to finish etc. Ideally though, it should be able to be calm too. On some occasions, that is the only side to work and it can be very frustrating learning to calm it down and let it release control for a while. Whatever happens, it is very personal.

Meditation is stilling the mind so that such things as wisdom, ideas, inspiration or healing energies may enter it. It can be experienced as a very dreamy state, similar to that which may be felt when day dreaming, stroking a cat or brushing hair.

The body needs to be relaxed and this can be a difficulty in stressful times. You may need to tense all the muscles first, in order to help relax them. If you cannot relax even then, perhaps taking up a physical activity such as swimming will help in the longer run.

Breathe deeply and easily, drawing the breath far into the body. Expand the stomach muscles as you breath in and push out with them as you exhale. (This helps to tighten tummy muscles too!) Imagine your breath as a visible object and concentrate on that until all the clutter has moved away from the front of your mind. If unwanted thoughts intrude, I usually give them some space and then tuck them away. If they are good ideas, I make a note of them. You could even keep a piece of paper and pencil handy, because there can be inspiration on the most odd subjects sometimes!

Some people prefer to look at an object, such as a plant, a crystal or a crystal ball instead. The idea is to quiet and still the mind and release it from its everyday clutter.

This in itself is very restful for the mind and body. I know that a short time of meditation is said to be worth several hours sleep, but personally, I like the sleep too!

It may be that ideas may enter the mind during meditation or the changes could be more gradual, but after a period of regular meditation, changes will start to occur in yourself and your life. These will vary from person to person and according to what they have stated they wish their meditation to help them with. Dreams may become more vivid and easier to understand. Events in everyday life may take on an extra dimension, perhaps functioning as signs and omens which can be interpreted. There may be an increased sensitivity to Earth energies or to other people's moods! Some people will use their meditation to consciously enter other worlds within themselves. Even if life does not become filled with wonders, you will be "making your mark" as a spiritual being. It all helps.

It may well be advisable to place a protective sphere around yourself when working, but whether you wish it to be a working circle, a protective boundary that is placed around your home anyway or something smaller and personal is up to you. You may also wish to pray and request protection from your choice of deity too. Many people will request the presence of the elements, but remember to thank them and release them afterwards.

This peaceful state of mind is also very good for prayer, but remember, prayer is asking, whilst meditation is listening! The answer may take some time to arrive too!

Meditation and silent prayer may give the appearance that nothing is happening, but in reality, they are very potent. Things are taking place on the other levels of life, but they will return to this world in some form.

All those monks and nuns who have shut themselves away for years, meditating and praying were not just making liqueurs you know!

Meditation is a very real force and something to find time for in a busy world.

Furthers listening:

The Spirit Seeker Meditation Tape One. "Essential Meditations - Grounding And Connecting and Tree Meditation" by Steve Hounsome

2. Find Your Own Space

There are many things which can be done indoors and in pouring rain, or when the children are asleep upstairs or when you live in a built up area and it is the middle of the night, it is often the best place available to work.

You can add so much more to your understanding though if you also find somewhere to work outside.

We may all dream of a wonderful secluded spot, preferably with a mature oak tree and water nearby, where we can work the most wonderful rites uninterrupted. Many of us have to settle for less a great deal of the time!

If you live in or can travel to a secluded natural area and enjoy its benefits, then you are indeed fortunate. Perhaps it is only possible on occasions, in which case you may have to store up your impressions to keep you going for a while! When you travel to a place which is unusual and interesting, see if you can steal away for a little time on your own. A moment by an old oak tree or a great rock or a stream can be a lifelong experience to treasure. You may be with like minded people who can share these quiet moments, but if not, try to get a little time to yourself.

A garden can have the most wonderful atmosphere though and it is possible to build a feeling of relationship with it. I do not just mean having a nine or eighteen feet circular patio or lawn, with a pond in the west and a barbecue in the south! (Though there is no reason why you should not!).

You can give yourself a surprising amount of privacy in a small garden using climbers and supports in addition to trees and fences. It does depend though on whether you wish to sit and meditate quietly or have all your friends round for a monthly shindig! Once people have decided you are acceptable as neighbours, they are decidedly calm about unusual behaviour in some places. Jon was building flint pillars to support roses and honeysuckle. We were quite surprised when our neighbours quietly enquired as to whether it was "some sort of deity?".

If you do have a garden, seriously consider both wildlife gardening and organic gardening. Not only can you help to reduce the poisoning of our planet and help a few wild creatures survive, but you will be bringing a little of the natural world closer to yourself. It is all very well invoking

dragons and great white buffalo, but why not make a pond for the frogs or encourage a few bluetits with peanuts?

You can fasten the birdfood near the window even if dwelling high up in a flat. It seems there are cases where birds will regularly visit balconies on high rise flats. One thing to mention here, it will take the birds some time to find the food if they are not used to finding it there. If your garden is full of berries and plants useful to them and all your neighbours feed them too, it could look like a Disney film very fast! Otherwise, be prepared to wait a few days.

Since the dear little old lady/wise woman/cunning man is not always to hand nowadays, it may be necessary to invest in a few books to gain your natural lore to help you to appreciate and understand the observations made. (If books are too expensive to buy, use the library system, assuming the Government have not cashed it in yet.) The travelling libraries can be amazing too, if you are at home during the day, one may pass near you and the staff will often go to enormous trouble to fill the shelves with the kind of books you are interested in. I should know! The van that comes by here now has a growing New Age and psychic section!

In the same way, the corner of a park, a particular tree or shrub, or even a group of flowers may have that little extra something to add to your sensitivity and help you to benefit from being there.

If you cannot go outside, then bring some of nature inside! Buy and love a houseplant or two, or nearly one hundred. (I say that, because in answer to my husband's comment that I had rather a lot of house plants, I counted them one year and discovered that I had ninety four containers in the house, some holding more than one plant!) When I lived with my parents, I had forty plants in my bedroom and even

grew runner beans in it one year! (No, I was not asphyxiated at night either.) If you are afraid that you will kill a houseplant, go to a good place that sells them and ask for advice. Making a good choice will depend upon whether your flat or house is cold or centrally heated, if you tend to water things all the time, (watering too much is the main cause of houseplant death) or whether you will forget it for weeks at a time, whether you are away a lot and how much room you have. You also need to really like the plant! I have a very strong feeling of personality from many of my plants and therefore, even though the house is over full at present, I could not bring myself to part with one of my old friends.

Let us assume that on some occasions at least, you are able to work outside. There can be another problem here, one of personal safety, especially for women. It can be far safer to go out in a group, or at least, to have a friend with you. Sometimes a friend or partner is willing to stand guard a way off, so that an individual can work in private, but with help at hand in case of problems. It is sad to think that the way that I roamed as a child (not so long ago), for miles through fields and woods, collecting flowers as I went in the spring and summer, have now become things we dare not do. It is not safe to let a child roam and the wild plants are protected now by law because they have become rare. So much for civilisation.

There may be one special spot to which you choose to return and which you will see change through the seasons. It is possible to show that you care for this place by performing such simple acts as taking along a carrier bag and collecting litter. You might like to leave small gifts such as flowers there too, but beware of poisonous varieties.

It is interesting to see how many public Pagan sites are filled with simple offerings. I have seen quite "ordinary" seeming people inspired to pick a wild flower or write a message and offer it along with the other tokens. Flowers are often present at Wayland's Smithy and West Kennet Long Barrow and the railings of the King Stone at the Rollright Stones had a branch attached to the railings with many little messages tied to it. They were being added to by members of the public.

The old Pagan wells were renamed after saints, but people still came with their offerings and tokens. Paganism is not far below the surface in so many people. No wonder established religion is so afraid.

You do not need to feel that there is only one place that you can become acquainted with. Different sites will feel right for different occasions. You might chose a place high on a hill to watch the Midsummer sun rise, a place surrounded by hawthorn blossom to celebrate Beltaine, a garden full of flowers for a handfasting and an old barrow for Samhain.

Always show respect to the place and its occupants, both physical and of other worlds beyond normal perception. In time, they may reveal themselves to you. Also, be careful who you tell about such a place when you find one. There are some people who really do not care.

I know of a place with ancient associations, ancient beech and oak, ash and hawthorn, with water nearby. It was so annoying (to put it mildly) on visiting it one day, to find that a great bonfire had been built right by the sacred trees, scorching their leaves. Also, the fireplace had been filled with broken glass and beer cans, (which some idiots seem to think will burn) and surrounded by empty cigarette packets and other debris. I doubt that such people would call themselves Pagan, I certainly would not! Some people call going into the wild and sitting around a fire whilst making an awful noise, Shamanism. If they have no sensitivity to the place, the plants and the animals that live there, there are a few other things one could call it too! There are people who are sensitive and insensitive under every banner, of course.

The fact that a thoughtful Pagan group did know the site was evidenced by the faintest of scorch marks in the grass, where their fire pot had marked the grass by the water's edge. (I know of one group using an old metal dustbin lid to hold a discreet fire. I hope I do not get turned into a frog for giving away that secret!)

Do try not to get into too many punch-ups if you discover yourself sharing a site! Most people seem to be quite reasonable if others treat them pleasantly. I have known a group wait quietly round a corner for others to finish, or agree to use a different part of the same site. Just occasionally someone gets possessive. There are sometimes queues for some of the major sites, especially at full moon and major festivals and as Paganism grows, other sites will find themselves used more often too!

3. Become more sensitive to Nature and the seasons

In the past, people did not need to learn to become sensitive to Nature. They were too busy being made wet by it, or too hot or cold. They spent their time carrying collected firewood through it and shoveling it off their paths and from around their front door and trying to find the sheep in it. They tried to store their crops through it and to make their hay before rain ruined it. They were too busy living with it to worry about being sensitive! We actually have this odd situation now where "cultured" people visit unsophisticated parts of the world and try and explain to the local people how wonderful their surroundings are, before someone bulldozes the lot!

Living with Nature does not necessarily mean you are sensitive to it, especially if most of your energy goes into just surviving, but for many, where life is not that harsh, there is some sort of chance of having a feeling for what is going on during the seasons.

We seem to have gone to an absolute extreme of cutting ourselves off. There are buildings where people work all day without seeing outside, even through a window. There are cities where flats and places of work are linked by underground trains, so that people never step out into fresh air. It fills me with horror. How grey souls must become and how easy to manipulate in that false atmosphere.

Even in our seeming deserts of concrete though, there are little oases of greenery. I remember again walking down that city street in which just one buddleia bush pushed up through the concrete. On it were all those sparrows, all shouting away. In another town, they were calling from the ivy on the side of a house. We had a pair who nested under a loose tile on our roof. Insects such as ants and ladybirds and beetles crawl around. There are even foxes and deer in towns these days. Nature will find its way in. How quickly a derelict site fills with plants!

Another thing which rather worries me is the word "attunement". When I first heard it, I thought it was something to do with a cure for a blocked nose. I found myself with a group of people and it was announced that we were going to do an attunement and I had not the faintest idea what they were talking about! Now normally I would ask, but things just did not work out that way, so people

132

stood in a circle and held hands and stood and stood and opened their eyes and peeked and saw someone else peeking so closed their eyes and pretended they were not peeking and fidgeted and peeked again and I realised that most of the people there had no idea what on earth we were supposed to be doing either! The person supposed to be leading this was quite unaware of what was going on. This was not a good example of attunement.

Attunement, simply, is feeling in tune with something, to be sensitive to it, to have a feeling of empathy. Ideally, I guess, one should be vibrating at the same wavelength as it, but that is pretty complicated, so let us just say that being observant and understanding makes a good start.

Being attuned is the sort of thing that lovers do automatically, in between the other bits, that is. I mean the bits where they are not talking because he did not wear both the ties he was given on Christmas morning and she has almost forgiven him when he foolishly admits that he is not too sure about lime green and purple and cerise and orange as colour combinations. The attuned bit is in between those. It is the bit where they stare into each other's eyes and both start smiling or laughing or humming the same tune at the same time and frankly can be almost as bad.

It is important to go out, sometimes into Nature and experience Her. It may simply be walking through the falling snow or getting a (rather large!) breath of fresh air on a blustery day. It might be finding your own tiny piece of wilderness for an hour or so or even camping alone on Dartmoor for a few nights. (Go well prepared! There is little New Age fluffiness about suffering from exposure.)

When you get there, do not just sit down and carry out a carefully planned ritual involving some distant foreign deity. Look at where you are and really appreciate it. Look at the trees and the rocks and feel the wind. Look at the animals, even tiny ones. You have entered their home. These things may completely change the way you feel and alter what you wanted to do. Places can help to calm you and help to give you energy. You must relax though, to what they are and what they offer and you must give of yourself too. You may feel that you get nothing from a place, but you must give feelings of love. Then something may or may not return that you feel at the time, but something will have passed between you. People think that they can take from a place and a great many things are given, but we must give too.

We expect to look at the animals. It can be quite strange when you realise that they are watching you. They have probably been far more aware of you, your sight, your smell, all the clumping great noise you made, than you have of them.

A neighbour of ours moved here from a less rural area, I believe. Having just been here a short while he said, "There is not much wildlife around here." I think he would change his mind now. We would certainly not agree! There are the bats, which he noticed his cat watching and the fox who comes too close for comfort, with us keeping chickens. There are hedgehogs, squirrels, mice, voles, shrews, rabbits and rats. There are hawks, owls, pheasants, rooks, woodpeckers, woodpigeons and collar doves, blackbirds, thrushes, wrens, robins, chaffinches, sparrows and all the little birds that look like sparrows, bluetits, great tits, greenfinches and starlings. There are frogs, toads, dragonflies and all manner of little creatures in our pond. There are many, many, butterflies (including peacock, red admiral and

tortoiseshell) spiders and insects (ladybirds, bees, wasps, groundbeetles, woodlice,) that would just take so long to mention that you would have to skip read the section. Then of course, there was the swan that landed on the road the other day....

The thing is, that quite often, we just are not aware of them. Try not only to look for these creatures yourself, but to be aware of them looking at you! Often, when an animal regards you with a calm interest it can be quite unnerving. It may be that there is a feeling of a message being passed to you and you have to spend time thinking about what has happened and how that particular animal and the experience relate to you.

I remember years ago, having risen very early one morning due to the attempt to camp overnight being disastrous. (Things did not bode well when I received a phone call at home earlier that day, from where we were camping, asking me how to erect a tent I had never seen! When I got there, the tent was hanging limply downwards. It had been tied to a tree by the guy ropes. That was it. It got worse, but I will not go on.) Anyway, thus it was that I was sitting on a farm gate at a very early hour in the morning when I had a very strong feeling of being watched. I turned round to find a hare, sitting just behind me and looking at me very intently for a long time. Eventually he wandered off and a short while later I saw him charging round madly, playing like a dog, in a field where there were long barrows. They were called the "Five Marys", but in line with tradition, there were six of them. I know this, because I went up the hill to where they were and counted them, several times.

In one of the visualisations I intend to put in my next book, I describe an encounter with three deer. These things can be regarded as a simple case of seeing a wild animal, but

sometimes they hit a certain chord within us which sets us thinking. On occasions, such a simple encounter can be a message which sets off a whole change in our lives. On others, it is just pleasant to see the animal! Do not expect every animal and walk in the country to change your life for ever! The rest of Nature has things it has to be doing for itself too!

Follow the seasons. You may be able to bring simple things back from walks, to remind you in your home. As usual, do not vandalise things, but trees drop leaves, acorns and conkers. If you cannot do that, then you may at least be able to buy a few seasonal flowers, such as daffodils in the Spring.

As the seasons change, things change psychically too and moods and emotions and states of health alter. Certain times of year may feel best to you, for certain things. Perhaps you always feel best in Summer? Maybe you love the Autumn. There are many theories about the psychic tides that change through the year. I will not go into that here, but just say, look at things for yourself. Do you have a fun time? An outgoing time? An introspective time? There may be a pattern from year to year as the seasons change.

4. Keep Records

Many years ago, few people could write. It was therefore somewhat unlikely that humble peasant folk would be keeping records of all their magical books. They would be slightly less rare than genuine coins with "100 B.C." marked on them.

There were still records kept though. They were in the mind and spoken to those they could be shared with. They were said aloud at rites. Some things were carved on sticks like tally sticks and the Cog Almanac, the old peasant calendar. Certain things, like tribal histories were committed to memory and told as stories or sung as songs.

Feats of memory for long sagas and the like, fill us with amazement. Yet, those minds were not filled with the terrible clutter of complete garbage that we have thrown at us. Television commercial jingles, the time of our doctor's appointment, the pin number of the cash machine, these facts jostle for space in our brains. We are time bombs of trivia, barely held together by a whole collection of stresses about forgetting.

Do yourself a favour. Make notes. Record how you feel at sacred sites. Write a description of a special tree that meant a lot to you when you first saw it. The ingredients for that incense that worked so well is worth keeping. That strange symbol you visualised just before you discovered all about psychic self defence the hard way is worth remembering. How did you feel when you first recognised the Earth energy rising within you?

You may be lucky enough to have been taught by someone who has a body of information, usually called a "Book Of Shadows" that you can copy from. You should also add your own material to this, even if you choose to keep it in a separate book. Speaking of books; I am sure there are some leather bound tomes out there in wonderful handwriting, but there are many ring binder files stuffed full of odd bits of information too! They have the advantage of being far more flexible, should you wish to add, rearrange or discard some of your collection. You could always put the "best" of your collection into a special volume.

Do keep these records safe though and be careful who you show them to. They are a treasure, based upon your innermost experiences. Make sure they are respected.

5. Dreams

Dreams are a learning experience which comes to you relatively free of charge. To learn from them, you need to be able to remember them, so it is a good idea to start to record your dreams. Some will seem far more vivid or important. They may be in colour, or even in a kind of "super colour" and you will want to take special note of these.

There are books which help you to understand dream symbolism. Check them first to see if they really suit you. Never follow one slavishly. It might be nonsense, or possibly, very good for others, but of little use to you.

If you have someone you can trust to discuss them with, it can be a great help. They do not have to be a great "Guru" with all the answers. (Such people are often idols waiting to topple in your mind anyway.) Friends who are pottering along trying to develop themselves as you are can sometimes help and the completely "uninitiated" often come out with marvellous pieces of commonsense wisdom too. You can gain wisdom all over the place, from a chat over the fence with a neighbour, or a child or an animal or a plant or even an otherwise banal advertising slogan.

I am not necessarily suggesting that you rush out to the dustman and say, "Last night, I dreamed that I turned into a fifty foot high carrot and this girl that I really fancy said she wanted to eat me. What do you think that means?" (Answers on a postcard..... No, not really..... I am joking!) There is this strange force which has been called

140

"synchronicity" and no one seems to have thought up a better word yet. Once it starts to operate in your life, it may become as regular and accepted a force as gravity. Believe it or not, once it starts to work, things that you really need to know will tend to be explained. People will mention it by chance in a conversation. You will switch the television on at random to find yourself in the middle of a programme on the subject. You will find a little second hand shop you had never noticed before and there will be a book on the very thing you were wondering about.

Let me give you an example. I was told that some of the stories that I was writing years ago were very like the work of a particular author and it was suggested that I should read them. It was not possible to find the work anywhere though. I could not purchase the book. I could not find it, even in a major city library.

After several weeks of searching, I entered a second hand book shop that I had bought from previously. I was rather surprised to find that all the books had gone. It had not been making a living it seemed and the owner had decided to change to antiques. The final straw was when a member of the public found a book which they said they had searched for for years and then argued over the price, claiming that its stock code was really the price and only wanted to pay a few pence for it. "All I have left" he said, "Is this one book which a friend borrowed and brought back after I sold all the others." Now, would you like to guess which book it was? When I told him how hard I had searched, he gave it to me!

Dreams are doors, not only to your subconscious, but also to the other realms in which you unconsciously dwell. If you wish to develop yourself, you need to take them seriously. You do not however, need to enter a useless ungrounded dreamy state in everyday life, or to exhaust yourself. Night time is also for getting your very much needed rest! If you find yourself tripping the light fantastic too often, you may need to give yourself a firm reminder that occasionally you are having a "night in" and are going to rest that night!

6. Events And Omens

Once synchronicity gets a hold and you learn to recognise it and not be afraid, then answers to your questions are not the only things which will begin to turn up, "out of the blue". To most people, this phrase suggests pure chance. As you continue further however, you will realise that less and less of what happens to you is chance.

Imagine a dew drop, hanging on the end of a leaf. There it is, a thing of beauty, catching the light, perhaps reflecting a tiny rainbow. It simply IS. However, the sun, the air, the leaf, all these things have acted upon it for it to be there. Now, the drop falls from the leaf and lands in a pond and ripples flow out from where it landed and a tiny ladybird on the edge of the pond, which was struggling and drowning in the water is lifted just a fraction and reaches a blade of grass and pulls itself out of the water.

Doubtless, the ladybird simply ambles on its way, a little damp. Had it a different kind of conscious mind though, might it not wonder if its guardian, ladybird angel had not made it happen?

Nothing is proved of course, it has simply entered the world of belief. I am saying though, that there may come a point where the "chances" in your life become so very regular, that you will have to bend your conscious mind quite badly to avoid seeing that what you have are interlinked patterns, not random events. The imagery of a web is very in fashion at present. What is causing or altering it, is a matter of faith. It is for you to decide.

People have always looked at seemingly unrelated events to help them understand their lives. The entrails of an animal might be said to give information about a battle about to take place or the flight of a bird could determine the successful outcome of a journey. Some of these things have entered folk superstition. A black cat crossing your path in this country, is usually thought to be lucky, (though some prefer it to pass from right to left) whilst in America, it may be thought to be a bad omen. On Portland in Dorset, men would go home and refuse to work in the quarry if they saw a rabbit and one should not even speak the word. This is said to come from a tragedy years ago when a rabbit warren had weakened ground which collapsed, killing workers below.

Other omens are largely open to individual interpretation, either through using psychic vision, remembering similar chains of events that have been linked before in one's life, or simply by following a gut feeling. There are symbols which have wider interpretations, but they may have a different meaning for you. It can be useful to keep a record of unusual events, much as you do with dreams. There is a limit to how much you can record though! Time is needed to get on with living too!

It can be of value to make a note of events which seem to exhibit synchronicity. When a name keeps cropping up from different sources and suddenly, that person chooses to phone you with an interesting new opportunity, is it chance or is it the web trembling?

Similarly, you might like to record occasions where you had an intuitive feeling about something and it happened. (Try doing it with things other than buying lottery tickets too!) Start to "play your hunches" more, but do begin with things that do not matter too much if you are wrong! Record the results and see if you recognise a pattern. If results vary, is it linked to the method you used to decide, the subject matter, what mood you were in or the time of month?

All in all, you want to become aware of the extra meanings of many of the ordinary things that happen around you. A firm base is needed to do this, however. Do not go completely over the top. Rationality and common sense are very important too!

7. Be Aware of the Otherworlds

Ancient people, such as the Celts, lived in a world which was permanently surrounded by and interlaced with other worlds. The majority of those living in the modern Western world have lost that understanding.

It has changed from a known fact of life, so accepted that one did not even think of it being otherwise, to a question asked on "Do you believe it?" type programmes, a half mumbled embarrassment when a culturally acceptable rite of passage, (births, deaths and marriages) is needed, or simply not mentioned at all. So great have been the many attempts to control thinking on esoteric matters and for so long, that many are left in a lonely vacuum.

The limited view of other worlds allowed to most people, (because to believe or think otherwise is "evil", or at best, odd,) has left a sterile gap in many people's thinking and yearnings. Those who have a working religious faith are fortunate, but, increasingly few it would seem in our culture.

Once that feeling of other worlds and other beings, not simply being there, but actively interacting with you in your own physical world is accepted, not merely as a rational possibility, but as something which goes beyond faith, a form of knowing, then life gains a massive series of new dimensions.

It may be that we are limited by our inability to see these other worlds, but if we also limit ourselves by refusing to believe that they exist, then we really are closing doors. In psychic investigations, it is those who did not believe in ghosts or whatever the phenomena being investigated, who are considered the best witnesses. Something has forced its way through despite their unwillingness to be convinced themselves. It tends to leave them in a severe state of shock.

(I do think sometimes that if this were carried into other areas of investigation though, it would bring odd results. If someone wished to prove that buses existed for instance, would they first eliminate everyone who regularly claimed to see and even travel on a bus as unreliable and self delusory?)

When other worlds are accepted, different cultures have viewed them in many ways and varied in their explanation. To some, all the non physical world would be seen as one vast area, others would divide it into sections, perhaps good and bad, upper and lower, cold and hot and to some, there would be infinite levels and worlds beyond ours. One is left wondering, does one get the afterlife one expects? (Start thinking good thoughts now. Have your Summerlands planned in advance!)

Similarly, groups will identify beings from otherworlds in accordance with their own views. A phenomena such as coloured lights might be seen as a fairy by one, an angel to another or a guide or an ancestor or an alien from outerspace or a nature elemental. Entire books can be written on these attempts to define the "impossible". Wars have been fought over differences of religious interpretation. People have been burnt at the stake because their angels were deemed to be devils. Within short spaces of time, opinions can change fashion in a most determined way too. People who see these things will react to them according to their own upbringing in addition to personal considerations such as curiosity and bravery. What one culture might be taught to respect and turn to for advice, another will run from in fear.

I do not believe that everything out there is rosy. There is a belief amongst those who have never experienced trouble, that you can think fluffy thoughts and all will be well. I have not found that to be true. There are things out there which are unimaginably good and wise, some real nasties and some which are really quite neutral when it comes to our own self importance. On the other hand, there is a great pool of knowledge and loving help which we can tap into and which is constantly feeding and helping us. Whoever we make contact with though, knowingly or unknowingly, we have to realise that we are always responsible for ourselves and that includes both making our own decisions and being responsible for our own safety.

Once someone finds their own way to an acceptance of that fact, then their whole life will change. They are no longer alone. There is help available. The simplest acts become linked to far wider horizons. A physical action, or even a thought slips out of this world, into the next and returns as change elsewhere. Recognise that? Yes, it is magic.

Magic, or other forms of otherworld intervention may take place as ordinary things, chances, synchronicity, coincidences and any manner of other thing that the determined can refuse to acknowledge as more than random happenings in a physical world. They may result in phenomena which are extremely difficult to explain away though. Heavy objects that move on their own, items that disappear and return in the most ridiculous ways, (often demonstrating a sense of humour), coloured lights, all these things could be seen as spooky, as most of us have been taught to be afraid of them. They can also be viewed as a possibly friendly and helpful being saying, "Hello. Are you ready to accept that I exist yet?".

8. Grounding, Centering and Closing Down

There are a great number of Pagans who are wandering around in an ungrounded, uncentered and dangerously open state of existence. This leaves them open to all kinds of problems. I do not think that many Pagans even really know what grounding means and that includes the ones who have followed courses, because even if the people running the courses understand it, those who are following them often do not.

People float around in a vague manner, thinking that if they feel all woozy, they must be doing it correctly. No, that is not correct. Helium balloons are wonderful fun. You have seen them bobbing around on the end of the string. Let go though and true, off they soar, but they are gone and you are left with an empty hand and often, a rather sad heart. (This may be rather more to do with flashbacks to childhood disappointments as much as the fact that they are not cheap to buy nowadays.)

I used to be very ungrounded. I used to find myself feeling floaty and dreamy sometimes. That might be alright in a wonderful field full of ripening corn on a hot summer's day. It was not so useful whilst doing sixty miles an hour on a motorbike or wondering which way up I was standing in the middle of a supermarket. (I think it was the humming of the refrigerators that used to set me off there.) Shopping can be difficult enough, without phasing out in the middle of a shopping centre or suddenly being so aware of all the different individual's feet and the pattern that they were drumming out, that I had to sit down to recover. Drunk? Drugs? Crazy? No.

Like a very large number of young people, I simply had no understanding of how to control a natural human ability that has been so suppressed for hundreds of years that, unlike learning to walk, speak or read, we are not taught how to do it. Despite the many, "My Grandfather was a werewolf" approach to hereditary claims, those who can claim to have been taught at the family knee are sadly few. In fact, so secretive are the genuine families, that their descendants often do not find out until later in life anyway!

It may well cause a certain amount of concern when your five year old child stands up at news time to tell her teacher and the rest of the class that last night her parents and eleven of their friends all took their clothes off to celebrate Samhain. It really did not bear thinking about forty or fifty years ago. (When I expect rather more clothes were kept on anyway, but then I do not intend to try and prove it!) Children frequently were not told. It was much safer. Rather than explain an invocation to the Goddess to a six year old, I suspect that "It is time for bed" "Get up those stairs" and "Mind your own business" were frequently what was said!

I discovered "grounding" and such things rather by accident. I spent quite a long time afterwards asking what had happened. Oddly enough, many very "knowledgeable" people did not know. One day in town, a gypsy came up to me. She gave me a "piece of information" of a very bland nature and then touched my arm. Unknown to me, this triggered off a reflexive defence mechanism. It was as if energy shot rapidly downwards, passing from me into the ground and then rose rapidly upwards through my body, out of the top of my head and from there cascaded down all around me. Now, I might have thought that this was all imagination, except that the gypsy took a step back and looked in a horrified manner, not at me, but about twelve to eighteen inches above my head. She really could see it!

Centering has been described by Starhawk as imagining that a pole extends downwards from the base of your spine into the Earth. You align your spine along that pole. Energy does indeed travel best when the spine is straight. You can experiment with this by meditating whilst lying on your back and then whilst curled in a ball lying on your side. You may find it more difficult in the second position. Slight shifts in movement may make quite a difference in your working in addition to your physical comfort!

The best way to understand centering, is to do it. The best way that I have found so far, involves grounding and connecting with "spirit" or Sky energy. I am sure there are others who would disagree or who would put this far better, but here goes...

I will try to describe it by saying that there is an awareness of the energy that courses through your own body. Then you become aware of the energy rising from the Earth and its relationship to you and then you become aware of Sky or spirit energy and you bring that into balance. If you add to that a feeling of where you are physically and balance that with a feeling of where you are outside of that time and place, within sacred space, then if you can calmly and gently bring those things together, you are pretty centred! I will recommend Steve Hounsome's tape again. It really is better to do it than try to read an explanation of it!

Another problem is that people are being encouraged to "Open up" all the time. So many want to be sensitive and are straining at the leash to develop themselves. The trouble is, that the world is not full of fluffy bunnies and rainbows. There are all kinds of people and beings and energies who will be delighted to make use of the vulnerable state this presents to the world and they may decide to latch on. It is a great deal more difficult to remove such problems than to have avoided their influence in the first place. Even without such attacks you have to function in the everyday world too. Floating around in a hazy manner where you are incapable of deciding which leg to put into your trousers first or are unable to make yourself a cup of tea in the morning is no use to anyone.

If you are consciously opening yourself, do so in good company that you can trust, use protection and close down afterwards. You may like to think of your energy centres with a protective magical symbol placed over them. Perhaps they are lights, which when closed down, you decide will cease shining outside yourself, with you in charge of the switch. Maybe they are flowers and the petals fold in. Just use whichever method feels best to you to tell yourself that you are closing down.

9. Protect Yourself

This carries on very much from the ideas above. You cannot develop your own sensitivity unless you know how to protect yourself in the everyday world as well as magical environments. Having the most sensitive hearing in the world might seem marvellous, unless you live near a motorway or have neighbours who like playing rock music all night!

I have mentioned closing yourself down. It is very 'in vogue' at the moment to form groups of a temporary nature and to open yourself right up with a group of complete strangers. The fact that this group may contain Attila the Hun, your local black magician, a psychic vampire and several severely unbalanced people is neither here nor there. Quite a few experienced and sensitive people, simply do not do it! They wrap themselves up very tightly. Now, this can leave one wondering, why people are there who are not able to partake magically. Why indeed? Open ceremonies can be great fun, but you do not necessarily get the best china out for a party where everyone is going to get roaring drunk. Do look after yourself.

You may also wish to think of your aura as strengthened with a protective bubble which you seal around yourself. If you find yourself in certain company that makes you feel uneasy or simply in a place that you do not like, these things may start to happen without you having to plan it.

Your protective bubble may strengthen itself without any conscious effort on your part, which will suggest to your conscious mind that a little extra caution is called for. Always listen to such warnings. We tend to believe that we can recognise evil when we meet it. It does not always come wearing a black cloak and hat or sporting fangs though! The sweetest seeming person might be harbouring several years of trouble for you. Pay attention to those intuitions.

You need to find the balance between believing blindly and inanely that if you think happy thoughts, everything will be wonderful and being quite paranoid! If you can recognise trouble and simply avoid it, you will save a great deal of energy and anguish.

Being well balanced and centered is another form of protection. A tree with deep roots is far harder to push over and a healthy body is far harder to infect. Similarly, someone who is happy and calm within themselves is far harder for another to latch onto or try to manipulate.

10. Give and Take

The "Take" side of things is badly out of control on this planet. I do not want to bore you with the lists of felled trees, unrecycled materials, etc. I hope you are doing a little something to tread lightly on the fabric of the great being who is letting us make an unholy mess of her surface in a great act of sacrifice to our development. I do not want to depress you with lists of poisoned water and air and endangered species. If we become despondent, we will lose the battle and we are not going to! There are people in positions of power who believe always in taking. They think they create riches. They do not. They create poverty. Many people are realising this.

Just think of all the ways that people are changing for the better. Think of litter recycling and keep saving things! Think of the "ordinary" people expressing their ideas about exporting live animals. Realise that some of the people arrested for protesting against road schemes are not just weird long haired travellers, but people like doctors, middle class, middle aged, middle of the road, "ordinary", you know, real people! Start thinking that way and you will be performing an act of positive magic without a candle or incense in sight. Though, if you happen to have some of that to hand of course...

Go to a site in the country and pick up litter. It does not have to be a recognised sacred site, just somewhere that could do with a little care. You can do the same in your city street. City gardens and all sorts of "impossible" schemes have come about because someone said, "This could be better" and rolled their sleeves up.

Yes. There are Earth healing rites and all sorts of magical rites which can be held, but you are in a physical body. You can do something physical too! If you pick up a piece of litter, you are changing the world just as much as if you enacted a ritual to bring about change. Magic, remember, is about change!

I am not forgetting about magical energies either. Some people go to a sacred site and they want to take away energy. They want to "feel the vibes" and become empowered. Go there and give. Give love. You will gain far more. Learn about exchange. You do not take, you exchange. Put that into action and you really will create riches!

11. Question Things

When I was eight years old, in a Religious Education lesson, I asked why scientists said the world took millions of years to make and "The Bible" said it took God just seven days. I was told that he did one thing on one day, then waited a few million years before carrying out the next action on another day. I am not sure, looking back on my school life, that I always did the best thing to be popular! I had a thirst for knowledge that can be frowned on by staff and pupils in the usual run of schools. My vicar remembered me for always asking questions. "It never quite clicked with you, Julia" he said some years later.

Many of those who have chosen to follow a nature based spirituality have studied the Christian teachings with more interest than the vast majority of those who automatically write C. of E. on official forms. They frequently respect both the original teacher and healer and his ideals. Then they have often continued their studies with Zen, Buddhism, anything they can find. Eventually, they come to something which has been suppressed by another religion for so long, often with lies and sometimes with terrible cruelty, that the claim that it is evil is very hard to override.

A feeling wells up from them, from their hearts and from the very land where they have lived. It links back over time and through ancestors and it feels right. There are so many, who when finally asking what Paganism is about, will say with surprise, "But that is what I believe!". Truly coming home is a wonderful experience.

Always ask questions. Never surrender yourself to what may become just another dogma. Always be aware of the absurd. Where there is mirth in your celebration, enjoy it. Do not let your actions and beliefs stagnate. If you ask why you are doing something and someone does not tell you, ask them why. Do not be stopped by, "That is the way it is" or "You are not yet at a level to know". (You were at a level that allowed you to think of the question though, weren't you!) Respect someone who says, "I do not know". I remember a school teacher saying, "I do not know, but I will find out" to me once. And they did. That is a person worthy of the name teacher. On occasions, you must find your answers elsewhere. A teacher who has your interests at heart will know this. It may be, that you will have something to teach back to them! Exchange again, you see. It comes in everywhere. Anyone who has ever tried to explain their beliefs to another will know how their own beliefs and ideas will be tested and grow in the attempt. The other's questions, often sparking off new ones in the teacher, like a series of small nuclear reactions.

Frequently, the problem in life is not finding the answer, it is finding the question.

Keep going. Have rests, enjoy yourself, take part fully in what you are doing, but be ready when the next set of miracles are ready to start unfolding in your life. A Pagan life suggests movement, development and change. If you stop somewhere and turn to stone, you have ceased to live it.

If you did stop, then, maybe, one day, along would come a question. What am I doing? Why have I stopped? How do I get going again? Once again, you will be off on that continual quest we call life.

12. Create From Your Own Heart

There are books of rites and books of spells and all manner of support ideas to get you going. You may belong to a group who organise for you or you may follow a correspondence course which lays itself out in a pattern, month by month. There should come a time though, when the flow starts to come from you.

Be prepared to work and speak from the heart. Let inspiration through. By saying this, I will upset all those who believe there are thoughts and rites and words that are engraved on tablets of stone, but I would think they grew annoyed with this book long ago.

If you are involved in a magical act, make sure you really mean it, otherwise do not do it. If you speak words, mean them. The simplest words which say what you really mean are worth more than the most high flown poetry, wonderful as it may sound. There are people who work with big words and set sounds and set pieces that have a marvellous history and that is how they work their magic.

I would say to you though, look also for the quiet magic, that which fits in the silences, that which creeps into your life like a tiny mouse. That which hangs on a web like drops of dew. That which whispers in the leaves. Find that magic and it will be with you all your life and throughout your life and beyond. If in anyway I have helped you to find that, I would feel proud to have helped you discover the flow of a wonderful magic, but most of all, you will find it yourself and within yourself. Once you have tapped into that current, you will never be the same again.

13. Respect Yourself

Be prepared to keep your own council. Born again Pagans can be quite a pain as they set out to evangelise the world! So can the, "I read one book so now I know it all" brigade. Apart from that though, there are those who simply will not understand your new ideas. They may not set up a stake and start gathering firewood, but you may find yourself suddenly rather lonely if you talk to the wrong people.

The vast majority simply do not understand about psychic abilities for instance, or are very frightened by them. You will have to choose your moments carefully, if certain matters are to be discussed. Consider the feelings of the other person. Are you saying something which will be of help or interest to them, or is it simply because you are bursting to tell someone!

Be very careful who you trust and always balance what they say against logic and your own inner emotions. If you take a strong dislike to a new acquaintance, respect those feelings, do not simply forget them. Keep them in mind. If they prove right, start to trust your own intuitive judgement more. Never allow your own pleasant and trusting nature to be used against you. It can be so easy for an "impressive" person to set themselves up to attract newly fledged Pagans and psychics. Be very aware of what are your ideas, your energies and what should be your own decisions. Do they help you develop your own power or do they suppress it or are they using it? I do not wish to create paranoia or megalomania, but be aware that if you genuinely develop your spiritual faith and your abilities, you will be holding a rare treasure. Be aware of its worth.

The last thing I will say, is to respect yourself and your own beliefs and desires. Listen to yourself until you understand your different voices. Recognise all the different aspects of self that lie within you. Recognise the frightened child's voice ("It might all go wrong") and the egomaniac's voice, (the one that says "You are so clever, look no hands!" just before everything topples).

Recognise most of all, your quiet calm voice, that which really does seem to know what is going on. It is from there that you will develop your contact with your Inner Self, Higher Self, Guide, Inner Teacher, in other words, with that which you can contact from inside yourself which will help you to learn and grow, regardless of what name you may choose to give it.

May you feel the Blessings of the Earth beneath your feet and the Blessings of the Sky above your head and may your heart and spirit continue to grow in love and knowledge.

Useful Addresses:

The Pagan Federation,
BM Box 7097 London, WC1N3XX

A fair sized Pagan group who wish to promote a more positive image of Paganism to the press and general public.

The PF publishes a magazine, "Pagan Dawn", previously called "The Wiccan", which covers news and items of interest and gives notice of Pagan gatherings around the country.

Originally Gardnerian in influence, it is spreading its cloak to try and cover all areas of the Pagan world.

"The Cauldron"

Long established and widely respected Journal Of The Old Religion, please do NOT write "The Cauldron" on the envelope.

Mike Howard, Caemorgan Cottage, Caemorgan Road, Cardigan, Dyfed, SA43 1QU

The Order Of Bards Ovates And Druids

O.B.O.D. PO Box 1333, Lewes, East Sussex, BN7 32G

Modern Druids who care about spiritual matters and the fate of the planet. Courses and training available.

Gippeswic

Pete Jennings, B.M. Gippeswic, London, WC1N 3XX

A magazine of the Norse tradition which is friendly and full of good humour.

Dragon Environmental Group

Dragon, No.3 Sanford Walk, New Cross, London, SE14 6NB

An environmental group with a magical and Pagan base. It has a newsletter and activities to help save the land, both esoteric and practical.

All Pagan organisations appreciate an SAE when you contact them.

Bibliography And Further Reading

Baines, Chris, "How To Make A Wildlife Garden" Elm Tree Books/Hamish hamilton Ltd 1985

Beswick, Francis, "Traditional British Honey Drinks" Heart Of Albion Press 1994

Beth, Rae, "Hedgewitch" Robert Hale Ltd 1990

Brodie, Jan, "Earth Dance" Capall Bann 1995

Brodie, Jan, "Magical Incenses And Perfumes" Capall Bann 1995

Brodie, Jan, "Psychic Self Defence-Real Solutions" Capall Bann 1995

Buckland, Raymond, "The Tree-The Complete Book Of Saxon Witchcraft" Samuel Weiser 1974

Cunningham, Scott, "Cunningham's Encyclopedia Of Magical Herbs" Llewellyn 1985

Cunningham, Scott, "Magical Aromatherapy" Llewellyn 1989

Davis, Marion, "The Magical Lore Of Herbs" Capall Bann 1994

Farrar, Janet & Stewart, "Eight Sabbats for Witches", Robert Hale 1981

Farrar, Janet and Stewart, "The Witches Way", Robert Hale 1984

Giordan, Marion, ed. "The Victorian Book Of Dreams" Hugh Evelyn 1964

Green, Marion, "A Witch Alone" The Aquarian Press 1991

Howard, Michael, "Angels & Goddesses, Capall Bann 1994

Howard, Michael, "The Sacred Ring", Capall Bann 1995

Heselton, Philip, "Secret Places Of The Goddess" Capall Bann 1995

Hindman Miller, Gustavus, "The Wordsworth Dictionary Of Dreams" Wordsworth Editions 1994

Hopkins, Cathy, "The Joy Of Aromatherapy" Harper Collins 1991

Hounsome, Steve, "Taming The Wolf-Full Moon Meditations" Capall Bann 1995

Hounsome, Steve, "The Spirit Seeker Meditation Tape-Grounding And Connecting and Tree Meditation" available from Steve Hounsome and Capall Bann

Jones, Prudence, "The Eightfold Year-Modern Invention Or Ancient Retention?" Capall Bann 1996

McArthur, Margaret, editing and contributions by Julia and Jon Day, "Earth Magic - A Seasonal Guide" Capall Bann 1994

MacLellan, Gordon The Toad, "Sacred Animals", Capall Bann 1995

Mickaharic, Draja, "A Handbook Of Psychic Protection" Rider 1993

Phillips, Matthew and Julia, "The Witches Of Oz" Capall Bann 1994

Ryall, Rhiannon, "West Country Wicca" Capall Bann 1994

Slade, Paddy, "Seasonal Magic - A Witches Guide", Capall Bann 1996

Starhawk, "Spiral Dance" Harper Collins 1989

Waring, Philippa, "Omens From Your Dreams" Souvenir Press 1991

Wilson, Steve, "Chaos Ritual" Neptune Press 1994

You may have noticed a slight bias to Capall Bann books in this bibliography. There are several reasons for this. I seem to have a very large number of Capall Bann books. (Several thousand.) They cover topics which I am interested in and discuss new ideas. Should there be an area which I wish to learn more about, I am in the nearly unique position of being able to ask a knowledgeable author to write a book on the subject. I also have the chance to read them before they are even published! (All jobs have their perks!)

Blessings - I wish you joy in your chosen path.

Steve Hounsome Meditation Tapes

From the author of 'Taming the Wolf- Full Moon Meditations', a range of excellent meditation tapes, using techniques and exercises proven in numerous courses. The tapes contain safe and effective meditations which can be used for personal and spiritual development, to promote greater awareness of the self or simply for relaxation and enjoyment.

Taming the Wolf - Full Moon Meditation Tape

This tape was designed to accompany the book 'Taming the Wolf'. Meditations are adaptable to the individual nature of each moon. Suitable for use at each full moon by groups or individuals.

Spirit seeker Relaxation Tape

Produced in response to an expressed need for physical and mental relaxation. Requiring no prior knowledge or experience, this tape is especially useful and effective for sufferers of stress, tension, worry, insomnia etc. It is also ideally suited to the maintenance of health and wellbeing during pregnancy, study and recovery.

Tape 1. Essential Meditations; a.. Grounding & Connecting b. Tree Meditation

This ideal beginner's tape gives a firm basis for all the other tapes in the series. People who have long had trouble with meditation, grounding and connecting have found it to be of great use.

Tape 2. The Sanctuary and Meeting Your Guide

Side one contains a guided visualisation which enables you to create and use your own special place or Sanctuary. This can be used as a place to receive healing or as a gateway to a deeper level of meditation.

Side two takes you back to your Sanctuary with the intention to meet your guide. It is necessary to become familiar with your Sanctuary first and the meditation may need to be repeated several times before you come fully into contact with your guide.

Tape 3. The Healing Ring and Purification Breath

Side one is designed to help with self healing. A ring is visualised which passes over the body, removing disease as it passes. It helps those needs of which you are subconsciously aware.

Side two contains a calming energizing and healing meditation. It is ideally suited to those in the process of cleansing themselves, perhaps by changing their diet or giving up smoking. It will also help you become more senstive to the needs of your body.

Tape 4. House Meditation and The Pink Bubble

Side one takes you on a guided journey which takes you to areas which symbolise your Mind, Body and Spirit and also your conscious, subconscious and every day selves. Symbolic items can be moved from one part of yourself to another.

Side two contains a visualisation which can help you to achieve your goals. It also helps you to understand them and how they change. A suitable symbol is visualised, enclosed in a pink bubble and released to the Universe.

Price £6.00 (inc VAT) + £1.00 p&p (within UK) Direct from Capall Bann
Freshfields , Chieveley, Berks, RG20 8TF

FREE DETAILED CATALOGUE

A detailed illustrated catalogue is available on request, SAE or International Postal Coupon appreciated. Titles are available direct from Capall Bann, post free in the UK (cheque or PO with order) or from good bookshops and specialist outlets. Title currently available include:

Animals, Mind Body Spirit & Folklore
Angels and Goddesses - Celtic Christianity & Paganism by Michael Howard
Arthur - The Legend Unveiled by C Johnson & E Lung
Auguries and Omens - The Magical Lore of Birds by Yvonne Aburrow
Book of the Veil The by Peter Paddon
Call of the Horned Piper by Nigel Jackson
Cats' Company by Ann Walker
Celtic Lore & Druidic Ritual by Rhiannon Ryall
Compleat Vampyre - The Vampyre Shaman: Werewolves & Witchery by Nigel Jackson
Crystal Clear - A Guide to Quartz Crystal by Jennifer Dent
Earth Dance - A Year of Pagan Rituals by Jan Brodie

Earth Magic by Margaret McArthur
Enchanted Forest - The Magical Lore of Trees by Yvonne Aburrow
Healing Homes by Jennifer Dent
Herbcraft - Shamanic & Ritual Use of Herbs by Susan Lavender & Anna Franklin
In Search of Herne the Hunter by Eric Fitch
Inner Space Workbook - Developing Counselling & Magical Skills Through the Tarot
Kecks, Keddles & Kesh by Michael Bayley
Living Tarot by Ann Walker
Magical Incenses and Perfumes by Jan Brodie
Magical Lore of Animals by Yvonne Aburrow
Magical Lore of Cats by Marion Davies

Magical Lore of Herbs by Marion Davies
Masks of Misrule - The Horned God & His Cult in Europe by Nigel Jackson
Mysteries of the Runes by Michael Howard
Oracle of Geomancy by Nigel Pennick
Patchwork of Magic by Julia Day
Pathworking - A Practical Book of Guided Meditations by Pete Jennings
Pickingill Papers - The Origins of Gardnerian Wicca by Michael Howard
Psychic Animals by Dennis Bardens
Psychic Self Defence - Real Solutions by Jan Brodie
Runic Astrology by Nigel Pennick
Sacred Grove - The Mysteries of the Forest by Yvonne Aburrow
Sacred Geometry by Nigel Pennick
Sacred Lore of Horses The by Marion Davies
Sacred Ring - Pagan Origins British Folk Festivals & Customs by Michael Howard
Secret Places of the Goddess by Philip Heselton
Talking to the Earth by Gordon Maclellan
Taming the Wolf - Full Moon Meditations by Steve Hounsome
The Goddess Year by Nigel Pennick & Helen Field
West Country Wicca by Rhiannon Ryall
Witches of Oz The by Matthew & Julia Phillips

Capall Bann is owned and run by people actively involved in many of the areas in which we publish. Our list is expanding rapidly so do contact us for details on the latest releases. We guarantee our mailing list will never be released to other companies or organisations.

Capall Bann Publishing, Freshfields, Chieveley, Berks, RG20 8TF.